AMERICAN
HORSEPOWER

100 YEARS OF GREAT
CAR ENGINES

MIKE MUELLER

First published in 2006 by Motorbooks, an imprint of
MBI Publishing Company, Galtier Plaza, Suite 200, 380 Jackson
Street, St. Paul, MN 55101-3885 USA

MBI Publishing Company titles are also available at discounts in
bulk quantity for industrial or sales-promotional use.
For details write to Special Sales Manager at MBI Publishing
Company, Galtier Plaza, Suite 200, 380 Jackson Street,
St. Paul, MN 55101-3885 USA

ISBN-13: 978-0-7603-2327-4
ISBN-10: 0-7603-2327-5

Editor: Lindsay Hitch
Designer: Amy Van Ert

Printed in China

Library of Congress Cataloging-in-Publication Data

Mueller, Mike, 1959-
   American horsepower : 100 years of great car engines / Mike
Mueller.
      p. cm.
   Includes index.
   ISBN-13: 978-0-7603-2327-4 (hardbound w/ jacket)
   ISBN-10: 0-7603-2327-5 (hardbound w/ jacket)
   1. Automobiles—Motors. 2. Automobiles—United States. I. Title.
   TL210.M785 2006
   629.2500973—dc22
                        2006017040

On the cover:
The 1971 Dodge Challenger was available with the mighty
390-horsepower 440 Six-Pack V-8. *David Newhardt*

On the endpapers:
Duesenberg's classic Model J appeared in December 1928 and four
years later was treated to a supercharged eight that produced an
unheard-of 320 horsepower. Only 481 Model J Duesenbergs were
built; of these, 36 were supercharged SJ renditions. *Photo courtesy
David Kimble*

On the contents page:
The big oil-bath air cleaner atop this 1950 Rocket V-8 was an option
that year. A conventional dry-element filter was standard.

On the back cover:
(top) At 450 horsepower, Chevrolet's 454-cubic-inch LS6 V-8 was
the highest-rated engine produced during Detroit's original muscle
car era. The LS6 was an SS454 Chevelle option for 1970 only.
A 425-horse LS6 followed for the 1971 Corvette.

(bottom) Carroll Shelby put Ford's High-Performance 289 V-8
to good use between the fenders of his GT350 Mustang variant,
introduced in 1965. Shown here is a 1966 Shelby Mustang
small block, which relied on tri-Y headers to help pump out
306 horsepower.

Contents

Acknowledgments

So many people to

thank, so few pages . . .

The author's brothers, Dave Mueller (at left) and Jim Jr. (not at right), both of Champaign, Illinois, helped make this book possible, with the former being a bit more supportive than the latter.

First, but not necessarily foremost, come two of my three brothers, Dave and Jim Mueller, both of Champaign, Illinois. As usual, they were instrumental in finding photo subjects and also handled after-hour arrangements once the shutter work (nondigital, mind you) was done. Good job, guys. Other family members also lent support, including Kathy Young (sister) and her husband, Frank (no relation), of Savoy, Illinois, and my ever-present parents, Jim and Nancy Mueller, of nearby Champaign.

Locating photogenic engines for this book was no simple task, but it was made easier due to the efforts of many friends, some old, some new. Two former bosses of mine, Donald Farr down in Florida and Jonathan Stein up in Pennsylvania, both helped lead me in fruitful directions, as did former coworkers (at Dobbs Publishing) Paul Zazarine, Tom Shaw, and Steve Statham. Longtime comrade Westley Peterson, now with the Antique Automobile Club of America (AACA) in Hershey, Pennsylvania, will forever by my hero for initially opening doors I didn't know existed.

Michigander John Clor, who once foolishly doled out assignments to this humble scribe from his defunct desk at AutoWeek, also can best be described as "dah man" after helping me hook up with SVO Mustang source Marcie Cipriani in Montoursville, Pennsylvania. I can thank Clor too for allowing my antiquated Hasselblads and me onto Ford's equally defunct Special Vehicle Team grounds, where he was recently employed right up until my work there was through. With SVT now in the archives, he's presently busy following in his hero's keystrokes. Good luck with your new Mustang book, John; may it outsell all of mine put together.

Newfound best friends include Richard Balsley and Tom Read at GM Powertrain, Greg Wallace at General Motors' fabulous Heritage Center, and cohort Ron Bluhm, who single-handedly made it possible for nearly a third of the engines seen in this book to make appearances. Bluhm also introduced me to Steve and Pattie Constable (of Idea Design Technique in Detroit) and David Kimble, of Marfa, Texas. The Constables' fabulous photographic art commonly appears in GM press kits, as do Kimble's legendary cutaways, masterpieces familiar to car nuts everywhere. Various Kimble creations grace these pages thanks to Dave's kind generosity.

Additional thanks go the gang down at the Collier Collection in Naples, Florida, for allowing me to photograph Miles Collier's Mercer Raceabout: Scott George, Jennifer Tobin, Gary Packman, Jess Yarger, and Bill Miller. The same goes for my friends at Don Garlits' Museum of Drag Racing in Ocala, Florida, who made it possible to capture various Ford flathead V-8s on film: T. C. Lemons, Peggy Hunnewell, and Chris Bumpus. I shot an Offenhauser four-cylinder through the kind cooperation of everyone at the Indianapolis Motor Speedway Hall of Fame Museum: Ellen Bireley, Jan Layden, Terry Gunter, Gordon Shedd, and Charlie Powell.

A Packard V-12 photo opportunity came courtesy of Scott Campbell and Rock Patterson at America's Packard Museum in Dayton, Ohio. Jack Miller, at the Ypsilanti Automotive Heritage Collection up in Michigan, allowed me an up close and personal visit with both a Hudson 7X six-cylinder engine and Herb Thomas' NASCAR-spec Hudson Hornet. And the fuel-injected small-block Chevrolet V-8, 426 Hemi V-8, Z11 Chevy V-8, and Dodge Viper V-10 were all found at Floyd Garrett's Muscle Car Museum in Sevierville, Tennessee. Like everyone else mentioned here, Floyd and his loyal sidekick, Bob Hancock, bent over backward for me, as they have many times before.

Still other photo sessions materialized thanks to the assistance of various individuals. Jean Allan, of Southport, Indiana, directed me to Corvair-crazy Charles Brema in Indianapolis, who rolled out both his 1964 Spyder and a nicely restored "pancake" six-cylinder. Muscle car restorer Dan Jensen in Michigan sent me to the Chicago area, where I found Jim Lerum's 1970 Chevrolet LS6 V-8 all ready to drop into his SS 454 Chevelle. Roger Gibson rolled out Glen Hansen's 440 Six-Pack V-8 from his renowned restoration shop in Kelso, Missouri. And Pontiac "Cammer" enthusiast Jim Black of Papillion, Nebraska, put me in touch with Warren "Dee" Sherrow and his 1968 Firebird Sprint in Cary, North Carolina.

Research material and historical photography came from various sources, including Pontiac man Jim Mattison, his counterpart in Buick terms, Marty Schorr, and Tim Yost, director of marketing at American Specialty Cars in Southgate, Michigan, where Buick's ASC/McLaren GNX was built in 1987. Kim Miller at the AACA Library in Hershey once again jumped through hoops for me, as did the folks at the Detroit Public Library's National Automotive History Collection: Mark Patrick, Barbara Thompson, and Tom Sherry. My chapter on Offenhauser would've never gotten off the ground if not for the able assistance of racing historian Spencer Riggs in Indianapolis and archivist Donald Davidson at the Indy Hall of Fame Museum. Brand Rosenbusch (Daimler-Chrysler Historical Collection), Candi Burchill (Walter Miller Auto Literature, Syracuse, New York), and Jon Bill (Auburn Cord Duesenberg Museum, Auburn, Indiana) all chipped in, too.

Finally come all the other people who allowed me into their garages to photograph everything from crankshafts to complete cars. In general order they are: 1928 Ford Model A, Curt Ware, Mahomet, Illinois; 1933 Lincoln KB, Patrick Ryan, Montgomery, Alabama; 2000 Boss Hoss motorcycle, Rich McKinney, Urbana, Illinois; 1964 Chevrolet Corvair and 1964 Corvair Rampside 95 pickup, Billy Bruce, Tyrone, Georgia; 1909 Ford Model T, Joe and Betty Jeffers, Vicksburg, Mississippi; 1912 Ford Model T four-cylinder engine, Russell Potter and Brian Cress, Bismarck, Illinois; 1927 Ford Model T pickup, Bill Broughton, Willington, Alabama; Mercer Raceabout, Collier Collection, Naples, Florida; modified Ford flathead V-8 and Ardun Ford V-8, John Brown, Vintage Acquisition, Palm Harbor, Florida; Mercury flathead V-8 and flathead dragster, Elmer Lash, Champaign, Illinois; 1935 Ford, Sam Revelle, Ft. White, Florida; 1926 Duesenberg Straight-8 engine (in bare chassis), Allen Strong, Urbana, Illinois; 1934 Packard V-12, Steve and Susan Zumdahl, Mahomet, Illinois; 1930 Cadillac V-16 phaeton, Allen Strong, Urbana, Illinois; 1950 Oldsmobile Rocket 88, Gene and Marilyn Roy, Casselberry, Florida; 1952 Hudson Hornet NASCAR racer, Ypsilanti Automotive Heritage Collection, Ypsilanti, Michigan; 1957 Chevrolet Corvette (fuel injected), Milton Robson, Gainesville, Georgia; Chevrolet L76 V-8, Dave Harris, Section, Alabama; 1964 Chevrolet Corvair Spyder and Corvair six-cylinder engine, Charles Brema, Indianapolis, Indiana; 1966 Ford High Performance 289 V-8 and Ford 428 Cobra Jet V-8, Bill Sneathen, Cape Girardeau, Missouri; 1966 Shelby GT-350, Tom and Ruthi O'Brien, Tuscola, Illinois; 1971 Dodge Hemi Charger Super Bee, Ken Salomon, Danville, Illinois; 1968 Pontiac Firebird Sprint, Warren Sherrow, Cary, North Carolina; 1969 Ford Fairlane Cobra, Neil and Denise Montgomery, Tolono, Illinois; 1970 440 Six-Pack V-8, Glen Hansen, Chicago, Illinois; 1969 Dodge Super Bee 440 Six-Pack, Stuart Echolls, Lakeland, Florida; 1971 Plymouth GTX 440+6, Steve and Janice Wright, Decatur, Illinois; Chevrolet LS6 454 V-8, Jim Lerum, Crystal Lake, Illinois; 1970 Chevrolet SS 454 Chevelle LS6, Dr. Samuel TerBeck, Knoxville, Illinois; 1986 Ford Mustang SVO, J. D. Anderson, Vero Beach, Florida; 1998 Dodge Viper, Tom Sellers, Champaign, Illinois; 2006 Chevrolet Corvette Z06, Robert Lovelace, Acworth, Georgia.

Many thanks to all.

– Mike Mueller

Four-cylinder engines dominated the American market during the 1910s and 1920s, thanks primarily to Henry Ford's mass-produced Model T. In 1928, the ubiquitous Tin Lizzie was replaced by the Model A (shown here), with a bigger, better four-holer.

Giddy-up

America's latest, greatest gas-fired engines are the most efficient, most

powerful wonders ever seen on the automotive

front. But are they really all that new?

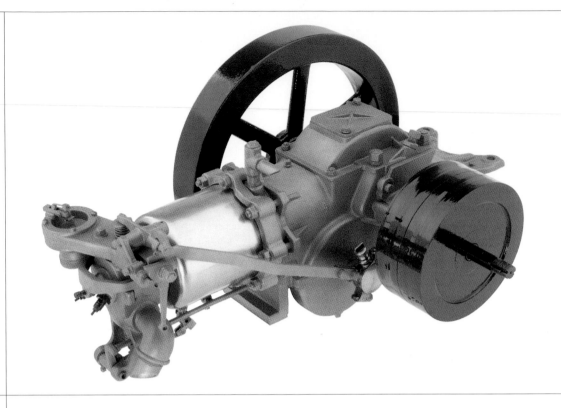

How simple things were in the beginning…. Cadillac's first cars were powered by this one-cylinder engine, which, in 1903, produced all of 10 horsepower. *Steve and Pattie Constable photo, courtesy of General Motors*

Times might have been hard during the early 1930s, but you sure couldn't tell by looking at America's most prestigious automobiles at the time, which relied on regal straight eights, powerful V-12s, and even outrageous V-16s. Lincoln's classic KB, introduced in 1932, housed 12 cylinders beneath its long, long hood. Shown here is a 1933 KB.

Compact V-6 layout? No, Buick brought the V-6 to this country in 1962. Turbocharging? Oldsmobile and Chevrolet's little Corvair introduced optional turbo engines that same year. Weight-saving aluminum construction? Buick pioneered the all-aluminum V-8 in 1961. Fuel injection? Chevrolet (and to a lesser degree, Chrysler) introduced fuelies in 1957. Hemispherical combustion chambers? Chrysler again, though its award-winning 1951 Firepower V-8 was a mass-production embodiment of a superior cylinder head design seen more than once many decades before. Overhead cams and four valves per cylinder? Most prominently Duesenberg in 1929. Roller lifters? Dual ignition systems? Tuned exhausts? Nothing new, nothing new, nothing new.

What sets today's marvelous multitasking powerplants apart from their countless ancestors are their computerized "black boxes," although electronic engine controls date back 25 years or so. Early electronics represented major advancements in the 1980s, but ever-higher tech upgrades have only recently maximized decent fuel economy and thrilling performance in integrated fashion at levels that were unimaginable not all that long ago. Traveling more than 20 miles on one precious gallon of gasoline in a car equipped with 300–400 horsepower is nothing to sneeze at. If only that gallon still cost 25 cents instead of $2.50. Price gouging and gridlocked gas stations? Also nothing new.

And to think it started so simply so long ago.

The internal combustion process itself dates back to Dutch-born Christian Huygens' experiments in 1673 using gunpowder as a fuel. Etienne Lenoir patented the first gasoline-powered internal combustion engine in 1859. German Nikolaus Otto pioneered the long-familiar four-cycle, or four-stroke (intake, compression, ignition, exhaust), engine two years later.

Duryea and Haynes initiated production of the gas-fed horseless carriage in America in 1893. Charles B. King, Henry Ford, Alexander Winton, and Ransom E. Olds then followed with their first automobiles in 1896. Starkly simple single-cylinder engines got Detroit rolling early on, and as late as 1903, Cadillac, Ford, Packard, Oldsmobile, and Auburn were still relying on primitive "one-lungers."

When Buick debuted for 1904 it did so with an opposed two-cylinder engine, as did Maxwell the following year. Locomobile had introduced an inline four-cylinder in 1901, followed by Packard in 1903. New, too, for 1903 was Franklin's air-cooled four-cylinder. Pioneered by Napier in England in 1904, the inline six was being offered by various makes in America by 1906, including Ford, Franklin, National, and Pierce-Arrow.

Push then turned to shove after Packard's new six-cylinder arrived in 1912. Late in 1914, Cadillac topped Packard's offering with two more cylinders arranged in two banks of four bores each opposed at a 90-degree angle—presto, America's first V-8. Packard returned the favor with this country's first V-12, the Twin Six, in 1915. Cadillac did its rival two better again in 1930 with an awesome V-16. Less never could be more back in those days.

Long, large, straight eights also came into vogue in the 1920s, with Duesenberg's introduced in 1920 and Packard's much more plentiful example in 1923. By 1925, straight eights were offered by the likes of Auburn, Roamer, Elcar, Jordan, Hupmobile, and Kissel. Buick's straight eight debuted in 1931 and was still running in 1952. Packard's last came in 1954.

There certainly was no substitute for cubic inches during the internal combustion engine's earliest decades. Raising rpm capabilities, and thus power potential, didn't happen until engineers developed mechanically operated valves. The first of these arrived around 1895 but only for the

Chevrolet's small-block V-8 is Detroit's longest-running, most prolific powerplant of all time. It celebrated its 50th birthday in 2003 and had powered about 90 million Chevy cars and trucks by 2005. It also has found its way into countless aftermarket applications over the years, including this Boss Hoss motorcycle, manufactured in Dyersburg, Tennessee, since 1990.

"Unconventional" was an understatement in the Corvair's case. Introduced by Chevrolet in 1960, this groundbreaking compact relied on an air-cooled, opposed six-cylinder mounted in back. The same was true for the intriguing Corvair 95 pickup truck, which followed its car-line cousin in 1961.

Some things old can be new again. Cadillac's first V-16 engine wowed the automotive world in 1930, and a second did the same in concept form some 70 years later. This 830-cubic-inch monster produced 1,000 horsepower beneath the 2003 Cadillac Sixteen's sleek hood.

intake unit. Perhaps the world's first successful production engine to feature mechanically operated intake and exhaust valves was the Mercedes four-cylinder of 1900.

Mercedes engineer Wilhelm Maybach devised a T-head layout for those valves—the intake unit was placed on one side of the cylinder, the exhaust on the other. Looking lengthwise inside the cylinder block, the engine's combustion chamber/bore area was shaped like a T. Competing ideas included the L-head and F-head. Also known as a side-valve engine, the L-head kept all of its valves in the block in a line beside the cylinders. Take the same lengthwise look inside an L-head engine and you'll see the combustion chamber off to the side of the bore, creating an inverted L shape. Last, and probably least, the F-head featured an overhead intake valve and an exhaust valve on the side. Much more common overseas, the F-head was comparatively rare in America and carried over after World War II only in Willys models. It was the L-head that dominated the American scene prior to World War II.

T-head devotees liked their design because its cross-flow combustion chamber apparently breathed better than other layouts, and thus T-heads were considered high-performance power-plants for their day. On the downside, a T-head required two camshafts compared to the L-head's one, and more moving pieces were never preferred as far as reciprocating masses were concerned. Multiple valves, on the other hand, have always been welcomed, and one of the earliest four-valve combustion chambers belonged to the T-head four introduced by Stutz in 1917.

Some engineers at the time, however, were convinced that the proven side-valve engine was the only way to go. As engineer Erik Delling wrote in 1913, "Fewness of parts is absolutely necessary in high-speed motors, and this is another reason why I am an adherent of the L-head motors. I could never see the reason for multiple valves and complicated overhead-valve mechanisms." In early 1914, Delling replaced Finley Robertson Porter, one of the T-head's biggest fans, as chief engineer at Mercer, which had been demonstrating this engine's prowess with its race-winning Raceabout since 1911. It was no coincidence then that Mercer dropped its T-head in favor of an L-head for 1915 and then quickly faded from American racetracks.

Granted, the overhead valves Delling spoke of did translate into more parts—pushrods, rocker arms, etc. But the OHV design also represented the best way to maximize efficiency. Dating back as early as 1903 in America, overhead valves offered various benefits, not the least of which involved a freedom to shape the combustion chamber in superior fashion. A hemispherical form, with a centrally located spark plug and valves inclined off toward their ports, was recognized early on as the supreme ideal. A. R. Welch may have pioneered the hemi head in America in 1904, and the Welch four-cylinder also featured a single overhead camshaft.

The OHC design made the OHV layout more palatable by deleting parts, most notably those pushrods. One overhead cam for both intake and exhaust valves was a great idea; two (one for the intakes, one for the exhausts) were even better. Wills Sainte Claire was one of the first American makes to try the single-overhead-cam (SOHC) design in 1921. Duesenberg used a dual-overhead-cam (DOHC) layout for its superstrong, 32-valve straight eight in 1929.

While Ford stuck with archaic L-heads up through 1953, its arch rival Chevrolet was an OHV proponent almost from the start. Introduced in 1913, Chevy's OHV four-cylinder was finally replaced by an inline six in 1929 with—you guessed it—overhead valves. And when Chevrolet's new-for-1955 OHV V-8 debuted, it set the American automotive world on fire.

General Motors pioneered the modern, high-winding, OHV V-8 in 1949 for both Cadillac and Oldsmobile, and from there an unbridled horsepower race was on. By 1955, Chrysler's Firepower V-8 was making 300 horses, and engine sizes were nearing 400 cubic inches as the 1950s closed. Auto manufacturers tried multiple carburetors, fuel injection, and supercharging during this decade to wring more and more power from Detroit's (as well as Kenosha and South Bend's) engines.

With the 1960s came two divergent schools of thought, as the great American muscle car took off in one direction and new budget-conscious compacts in another. At the same time, Chevrolet was building a 425-horsepower 409-ci V-8 and a polite air-cooled "pancake" six for its little Corvair. By 1970, Chevy's biggest big-block V-8, a 454-cube beast, was pumping out 450 horsepower in LS6 trim. The next year, Ford's Pinto was on the scene with its 75-horse, 98-ci four-cylinder.

High performance faded away after gasoline started turning to gold in the 1970s. Fast-thinking engineers, however, recovered and brought the muscle car back in the 1980s. The Big Three toyed with turbochargers during this decade, but the real advance involved trading carburetors for electronically controlled fuel injection. Ford's Mustang GT, with its 5.0-liter EFI V-8, especially made hay after the new technology arrived in 1987.

Nowadays, all vehicles are electronically injected, and many feature overhead cams and aluminum construction. Many modern V-6s put their V-8 predecessors to shame, but the latter engines too have found new muscles. Chevrolet's new-for-2006 LS7 small block is now offering 505 horsepower. Yikes.

Fresh, exciting engines are everywhere you look today, and out-of-this-world experiments just keep coming, too. But some carryovers remain. Chrysler recently revived its Hemi V-8, and Cadillac showed off a new V-16 concept—both engines proving without a doubt that everything old can be new again.

Chrysler Corporation too has decided to relive its legendary past. Both these 2006 Dodge models are powered by the latest rendition of the famed Hemi V-8, a power-packed design that dates back to 1951.

Ford's first Model T appeared in October 1908 as a 1909 model. More than 15 million more followed before the world's first mass-produced car was finally retired in 1927.

CHAPTER 1

Motor for the Masses: Ford Model T Four-Cylinder

Henry Ford always was stubborn as hell. He also was rich as hell, and he

didn't get that way by chance. Or did he? Was Henry

simply lucky that the Model T remained so successful

for so many years? Or was he really the only genius

in Detroit who recognized that mass-producing an

affordable car for Average Joe was the one really big

secret to automaking?

All Model T Fords featured four-cylinder inline L-head powerplants, which varied in many ways during the 1909–1927 run. But constant during those years was trendsetting integral construction: All four cylinders and the top of the crankcase were cast together in one chunk of iron. Shown here is a 1912 Model T powerplant.

Many of his decisions still have historians shaking their heads. Nonetheless, it was the Model T's record-shattering sales bonanza that rendered moot any further judgment of the man who brought us the mass-production assembly line. It's tough to argue with success, and it didn't come more successful than his Tin Lizzie, 15 million of which were built over almost 20 years. By 1921, Dearborn was rolling out more vehicles than all other manufacturers combined, and the company's fortunes had grown so huge the boss probably could've run things with a Ouija board and still stayed on top. But with modern progress seeming to matter so little to him, how could he have stayed so far ahead of the competition for so long?

Well, he didn't. And even after Chevrolet took over the industry's top sales spot in 1927, Henry Ford still refused to update many aging aspects of his products. Most often, he would defend his obstinate stance by pointing out that simplicity was Ford's strongest selling point. It didn't come much simpler than a transverse buggy spring, and that relic of the horseless carriage days amazingly still suspended Ford cars at both ends until 1949, only because Henry said so. "We use transverse springs for the same reason that we use round wheels," he huffed, "because we have found nothing better for the purpose."

Obviously, superior advances like hydraulic brakes and Hotchkiss drive also were ignored. Chevrolet began installing hydraulic stoppers on its cars in 1935, while mechanical brakes continued offering Ford drivers "the safety of steel from toe to wheel" until 1939, again by the boss's iron-willed mandate. A Hotchkiss-type open driveshaft didn't replace Ford's enclosed torque-tube drive until Dearborn's thoroughly modern postwar models finally arrived for 1949.

And, like the car it powered for so many years, Ford's diehard four-cylinder engine was allowed to get a little too long in the tooth before Henry finally made a change. "I've got no use for a motor that has more spark plugs than a cow has teats," he once growled during the Model T's heyday.

It's safe to say that, as American engines go, there was nothing all that great about the Model T four-cylinder—other than the fact that it reliably and economically powered the most significant car in Detroit history, if not the whole world. Introduced in October 1908 as a 1909 model, the first Model T was understandably honored in 1996 by *Automobile* magazine as one of "The 24 Most Important Automobiles of the Century," along with, among others, the fabled 1932 Ford V-8 model.

"In 1909, (Model T) production reached nearly 11,000," began *Automobile*'s honorarium. "In 1913, Ford produced more than 168,000, and America was suddenly on wheels. By 1918, half of the cars on the entire planet were Ford Model Ts. As productivity improved through Henry Ford's creation of the first moving automotive assembly line (in 1913), the price was cut repeatedly, making his simple, reliable car available to literally everyone." Nearly 70 years earlier, the *Boston News Bureau* had called that 1913 production total "simply phenomenal"—this after claiming that 1912's run of 78,000 Ts was "remarkable."

Though no one called the first Model T's four-cylinder L-head remarkable, two notable innovations did stand out. Unlike most engines of the day, which were cast with separate crankcases and cylinders (the latter units coming singularly or in pairs), the Model T motor was cast *en bloc*. Its four cylinders, as well as the top half of its crankcase, were produced all together from one piece of iron, and a superior piece at that. Henry Ford may have demanded cheap simplicity in his automobiles, but he didn't scrimp as far as metallurgy was concerned, and he had one of the industry's best minds in the field, Childe Harold Willis, overseeing that engineering facet.

Most engines of the day also featured integral cylinder and cylinder head castings, while Ford's inline four was crowned with a removable head for easy maintenance. More than one rival engineer claimed this separate cylinder head wouldn't work, that it would leak. But these fellows were left scratching their own noggins after the Ford design proved valid and soon became the industry standard. Reportedly, the first 500 Model T engines built used 3/8-inch bolts (13 of 'em) to hold their heads on, but these were traded for sturdier 7/16-inch bolts.

Early engines featured a water pump driven off the timing gear in front. But that changed after the first 2,500 four-cylinders were built, as the boss decided to switch to a simpler,

Opened in January 1910, Ford's huge, highly efficient Highland Park plant was already a wonder when the company's historic moving assembly line began operating in April 1913. Ford production doubled that year, then really got rolling in 1914, when about 1,000 Model Ts started leaving the line each day. The one-millionth Model T was built in December 1915. *Courtesy David Kimble*

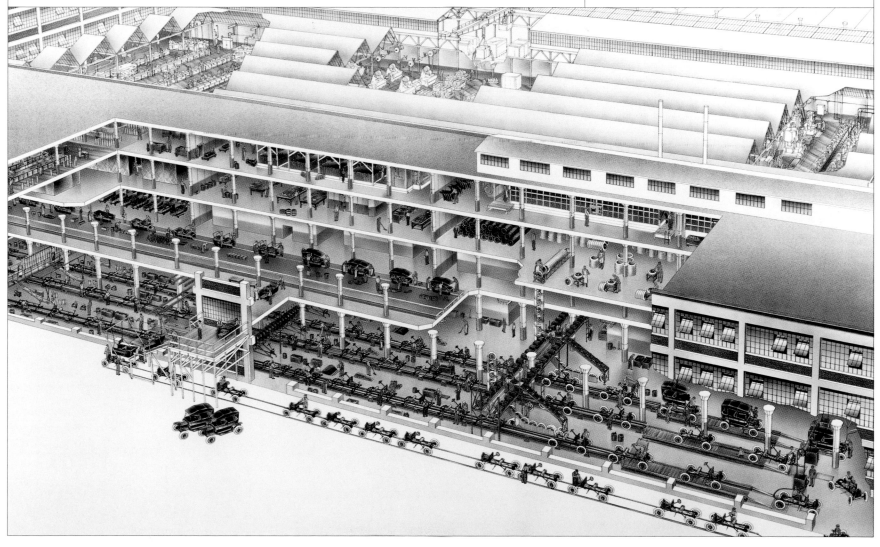

cheaper, thermo-siphon cooling system. Dropping the water pump meant recasting both the block and head (for extra coolant capacity), and various other revisions were required, including a modified timing cover, a relocated water outlet, and a belt-driven fan in place of the gear-driven unit.

The four-cylinder was lubricated by the simple splash method, whereby the connecting rods' lower ends dipped down into the oil supply and splashed it up into the block. Gravity took over from there. An innovative low-tension magneto incorporated into the flywheel handled ignition. Bringing up the bottom end, a pressed-steel crankcase cover also served as a lower housing section for the T's two-speed planetary transmission, essentially making the engine and gearbox one integral unit, all of it lubricated by the same oil supply.

Basically a primitive automatic transmission with mechanical-activated bands instead of the hydraulic control familiar today, Ford's planetary box used foot pedals and a lever to operate. Early Model T drivers found two pedals (for low and high speeds) on the floor and two levers. One lever was for braking, while the other worked the transmission's reversing bands. After 500 to 800 (sources vary) Model Ts were built, this layout changed to the famous three-pedal system, which featured one lever for the parking brake, neutral, and high speed. The three pedals operated low speed, reverse, and the driving brake.

The engine's bore and stroke was 3.75 by 4.00 inches, bringing displacement to 176.7 cubic inches. Maximum output was 20 horsepower at 1,600 rpm, more than enough oomph to move the 1,200-pound Model T briskly along like cars that cost much more. Compression was 4.5:1, and an updraft carburetor from Kingston, Buffalo, or Holley delivered fuel.

As was the case in 1909, Ford made running changes seemingly every year thereafter to the Model T four-cylinder, some notable, most trivial. Compression dipped more than once and displacement varied here and there by a tenth of a cubic inch or so. But most recognize the 176-ci displacement tag as a constant through the Model T run. Output also varied, though the same "20–22" horsepower tag remained up through 1927.

Left: Internal changes included exchanging the diamond-throw crankshaft (left) for a straight-throw crank in 1924.

Center: Cylinder head design changed during 1917, with the original low head replaced by this high head, which allowed for more room inside in the combustion chamber. This in turn translated into a lower compression ratio.

Right: The Model T's two-speed planetary gearbox was more or less a primitive automatic transmission that used mechanically operated bands instead of hydraulic pressure to control shifts. It too was updated during the Model T run, with one change involving a larger brake drum, installed in 1925. At left is the original small drum used from 1909 to 1925.

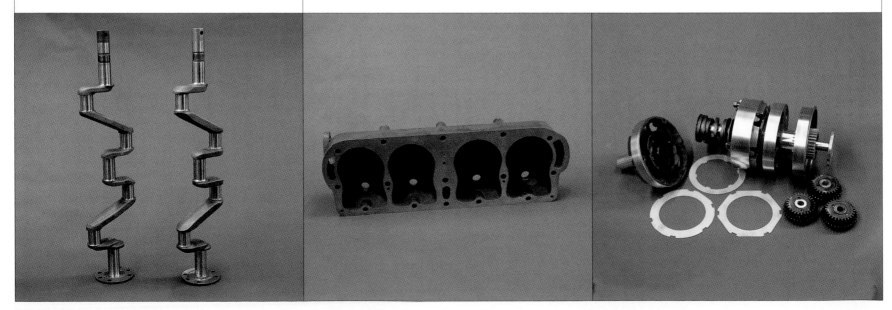

More important improvements included adding two steel covers for the previously exposed valve stems and valve springs in 1911. That same year, the crankcase and transmission housing were modified with openings for easier maintenance of bearings and drive bands, respectively. Ford added revised heads in 1912 and 1913 and cut compression to 4:1 by that latter year. A new camshaft with more overlap (for smoother running, yet less power) also appeared in 1913. With the popularity of electric lighting, Ford introduced a new magneto with larger magnets in 1915. Compression dropped again slightly that year, probably due to resized connecting rods.

A new, taller radiator replaced the old brass unit in 1917, as wartime metal shortages came into play. Ford engineers added a longer cast-iron hose nozzle to reach the new radiator and enlarged the heads to aid cooling. Compression again dropped, this time to 3.98:1.

Perhaps the most welcomed change came in 1919. Up until then, all Model T owners brought their cars to life with a hand crank. Cadillac had pioneered the electric self-starter in 1912, but it took a few years to filter down into the low-priced ranks. Ford's first electric starter came as a $75 option for 1919 Model Ts, but only for closed cars. That option changed to a standard feature (unless the buyer demanded otherwise) on coupes and sedans by midyear, at which time open Ts began showing up with the new system, once again delivered as a $75 option.

Along with an ultraconvenient starter motor, that electrical system included a storage battery, a generator, headlights, and taillights. Ford redesigned the engine block and transmission case both to mount these extra pieces and allow them to operate. The flywheel gained a ring gear to give the starter something to start, and a stronger timing gear went onto the camshaft to serve double duty as a drive source for the 6-volt generator. Ignition, meanwhile, remained the flywheel-fired magneto's responsibility, as it would throughout the Model T's life.

All Model Ts built later in 1919 received the updated engine block and transmission case, regardless of whether or not they had the new electrics, once stores of the old castings ran out. The starter system itself remained somewhat slow to catch on among the Ford faithful, simply due to cost. Rural buyers were especially hesitant, as most country folk were well acquainted with such rigors as cranking an engine and in no hurry to grow "soft" like a city slicker. But by 1927, all Fords featured convenient electric starters.

Another new block casting appeared in 1921, this one with a one-piece tappet cover in place of the two separate units used since 1911. Ford installed new lightweight connecting rods that year, followed in 1924 by lighter pistons and a revised oiling system. New quick-change transmission bands with removable ears came along the following year. Seemingly countless carburetors were seen atop the Model T four during its long run.

That run finally came to end in May 1927. Waiting in the wings for its 1928 introduction, the Model A had a bigger, better L-head four-cylinder, and Dearborn engineers were already at work on another milestone, the "flathead" V-8. Henry Ford may have been stubborn, but he wasn't stupid. We can only wonder how much longer his company might've dominated the industry had he just let himself recognize the winds of change.

By 1927, all Model Ts came standard with convenient electric starters, but a hand crank was still included as a backup. Ford first offered an optional electric starter in 1919.

In 1912 Ralph De Palma set eight new world class records with a Raceabout in Los Angeles.

MERCER

Mercer's original Raceabout was a stripped-down, no-nonsense machine built with one thing in mind: speed. According to noted automotive writer Ralph Stein, you didn't just get into one of these automobiles, you got on it.

CHAPTER 2

Racing Improves the Breed: Mercer T-head Four-Cylinder

In November 1895, the *Chicago Times-Herald* sponsored America's first

officially sanctioned competition event for the

newfangled horseless carriage, a 50-mile jaunt held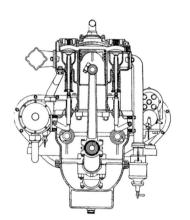

in the Chicago area, and from there the race was on.

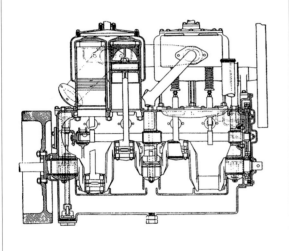

T-head engines got their name from the way the valve pockets traced out a T in relation to the cylinder bore when seen from a longitudinal perspective (below).

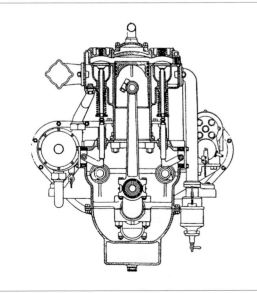

Pitting automobiles against each other in tests of speed, strength, and endurance proved to be just the ticket to convince potential customers that this new technology was viable, that they couldn't lose by shelling out their hard-earned dollars for a piece of the action.

Alexander Winton was among the earliest American automakers to reap real benefits from a race-winning reputation. By 1900, Winton, then America's third-largest automaker behind Locomobile and Columbia, was recognized as the hottest thing running in the burgeoning internal combustion arena. But in October 1901, a Winton was defeated by Henry Ford's first race car, a polite little jalopy that averaged a heady 43.5 miles per hour during a 10-mile dash. Ford then backed up this major upset with another win over a Winton in 1902, this time using a monstrous machine named after a record-setting New York Central railroad locomotive wearing the number "999." The rest is—you guessed it—history.

As Benson Ford explained in 1962, "At the turn of the century, my grandfather built the 'Old 999,' the world's first great racing car, and raced it with the immortal Barney Oldfield at the tiller, performing miracles unheard of in its time. The publicity from his racing efforts attracted the capital that enabled him to create Ford Motor Company."

Once up and running, Ford did all of its winning with the affordable, purely practical Model T, and it was years before old Henry's firm got involved in racing again. But many others were more than willing to fund competition teams during the decade prior to World War I, with the goal to "win on Sunday, sell on Monday." Though this adage wasn't actually coined until the 1960s, the basic idea is as old as the automobile itself.

Prime racing venues prior to the Great War included the likes of Ormond Beach, Elgin, Brighton Beach, Long Island's Vanderbilt Cup, and Mt. Washington's "Climb to the Clouds." Among the big winners at these events and so many others were the likes of Lozier, Simplex, Moon, Marion, and Chadwick.

But perhaps the most memorable moment came in May 1911, when Ray Harroun drove his Marmon Wasp 500 miles to a win at a 2.5-mile brick-paved track that had opened in August 1909 in an Indiana prairie 4 miles outside of downtown Indianapolis. Billed as "the greatest automobile race ever run in the history of the industry," this inaugural event was officially titled the "Memorial Day International Sweepstakes." Today, we simply call it the "Indy 500," long known as "the greatest spectacle in motorsports."

Early Indy fields were filled with modified production machines, as well as some entries that appeared as if they rolled right off Indianapolis' streets. In 1912, the second Memorial Day 500-miler was won by a local boy driving a local car—Joe Dawson in his Indianapolis-built National, probably the closest thing to a stock passenger car ever to turn a lap around the "Brickyard."

The year before, the first 500-miler had served as a showcase of sorts for a similarly stock vehicle built by a company from Mercer County, New Jersey. Named after its locale, the Mercer Automobile Company traced its roots to 1902, when William Walter rolled out the first car from his American Chocolate Machinery Company factory in New York. By 1905, Walter was being supported financially by the Kuser brothers, John and Anthony, as well as various

1911 MERCER RACEABOUT

Type: water-cooled inline four-cylinder T-head, hand crank starting

Construction: cast iron, two separate blocks of two cylinders each bolted to common crankcase

Lubrication: pressure and splash

Main bearings: three

Bore and stroke: 4.375x5.0 inches

Displacement: 300 cubic inches

Valves: in block; four intakes on right side of cylinder bores, four exhausts on left; 2.25 inches in diameter, made of tungsten steel

Camshaft: two in crankcase on opposite sides of crank

Induction: Fletcher single-throat updraft carburetor

Ignition: Bosch magneto, two spark plugs per cylinder

Horsepower: 58 at 1,800 rpm

members of the Big Apple's much more famous Roebling family. In 1906, the Walter Automobile Company was incorporated and relocated to a brewery building owned by the Kusers across the Hudson River in Mercer County; Trenton to be exact. But Walter failed, and in May 1909, it was superseded by the renamed Mercer firm, with Ferdinand Roebling president, his brother Charles vice president, and John Kuser secretary treasurer. In other pursuits, "Ferdie" and Charles' father, John Roebling, along with his other son, Walter Roebling I, had (with the support of the Kusers) built the Brooklyn Bridge.

Charles Roebling and his son, Washington Roebling II, were in charge of production at Mercer, and it was the younger man who was most responsible for the company's ventures onto the racing stage. Reportedly, Charles Roebling didn't care all that much for the newfangled automobile, but his playboy son was fascinated, not only with cars in general, but high-performance machines in particular. He wanted to build fast, well-handling vehicles that would both attract jet-setting customers and win races, further enhancing the image of other Mercer models that wouldn't necessarily possess competitive natures.

So it was that Mercer unveiled its Model 30-C Speedster in 1910. Powered by an outsourced four-cylinder L-head Beaver engine, this low-slung hot rod was both fast and rugged, quickly establishing Mercer as a force to be reckoned with.

Aiding that charge was Finley Robertson Porter, a dynamic engineer who joined the company in 1910 and instantly made his presence known. Like Washington Roebling II, Porter had a fondness for the sporting side of automotive engineering, and when the two put their heads together they created what was arguably America's first great performance automobile: the Mercer Type 35-R Raceabout, introduced late in 1910 as a 1911 model. Suspended as low as it could go, wearing only minimal bodywork, the Raceabout looked every bit like a race car: rude, mean, and nasty. As automotive writer Ralph Stein later put it, you didn't get in a Mercer Raceabout, you got on it.

The heart of the intimidating Raceabout was Porter's T-head four-cylinder, a 300-cubic-inch inline mill that, though rated at about 35 horsepower, actually put out 58 healthy horses at 1,800 rpm, enough muscle to allow a top end as high as 72 miles per hour for that 2,500-pound

Above, left: Mercer introduced its first Type 35-R Raceabout late in 1910 as a 1911 model.

Two Mercer Raceabouts were in the 46-car field for the first Indianapolis 500, run May 30, 1911. They finished 12th and 14th.

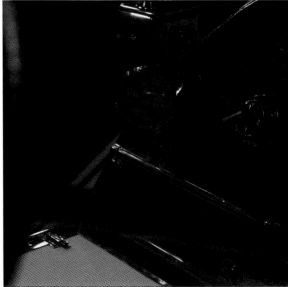

machine. Its cylinders were cast in pairs and bolted to a common crankcase, per existing convention. Three main bearings held the forged-steel crank in place, and oiling was a combination of pressurized flow and simple splash. Connecting rods were forged steel, while pistons were cast iron. A gear-driven centrifugal pump, located on the left side, handled cooling chores. Bore and stroke measured 4.375 and 5 inches, respectively.

In typical T-head fashion, the Mercer four featured two camshafts, one running down each side of the aluminum alloy crankcase, both gear-driven off the crank. The cam on the right operated the four intake valves; its partner on the left did the same for the four exhausts on the opposite side. All eight tungsten-steel valves were interchangeable, measuring 2.25 inches in diameter. Their stems and springs were exposed, and their tappets were activated down inside the crankcase by pivoting intermediate rocker arms that negated any side loading as the cam lobes did their reciprocating thing.

A gear-driven Bosch magneto, located up front on the engine's right, took charge of ignition. Each cylinder featured two spark plugs, one directly over the intake valve, the other over the exhaust. Firing was simultaneous, though a switch could allow one set of plugs to operate singularly. A Fletcher carburetor, also located on the right, supplied the air/fuel mixture through a compact intake manifold. A generously sized exhaust manifold on the opposite side of the block sent spent gases on their way. A three-speed gearbox originally brought up the rear, but it was replaced in 1913 by a much-improved four-speed unit.

All these parts together equaled a no-nonsense performance machine that couldn't help but attract adoring followers. As legendary automotive writer Ken Purdy explained it in his book, *Kings of the Road*, "To put the Mercer in its proper frame of reference, to understand its tremendous appeal for the motorists of its time, one must ponder for a moment the fact that strictly stock Mercers were often taken straight from the show room to the track."

Indeed, two stripped-down Raceabouts went to Indianapolis in 1911, and after completing the 500-miler (without once having to open their belted-down hoods), both were refitted with lights, fenders, and running boards and driven "home" from the track. Mercers entered six major races in 1911, garnering five wins, two seconds, and one third. More victories and speed records followed in 1912, including a third-place finish at Indianapolis, and Raceabouts continued punishing the opposition up through 1914. Mercer team drivers during those years included some of racing's best: Hughie Hughes, Ralph De Palma, and Barney Oldfield, to name a few.

But as successful as the Mercers were from 1911 to 1914, they couldn't beat fate. History first dealt the company a bad hand in April 1912, when Washington Roebling II went down

Top: Mercer muscle came from a 300-cubic-inch T-head four-cylinder featuring twin camshafts—one for the intake valves, one for the exhausts. Output was 58 horsepower.

Center: T-head advantages included a cross-flow design. This Fletcher updraft carburetor fed the intake valves on the engine's right, while spent gases exited the combustion chambers on the opposite side.

Below: Reportedly, a T-head Raceabout could top 70 miles per hour—heady speed for its day.

with the *Titanic*, taking with him the driving force behind Mercer's racing program. Two years later, Porter left to form his own company, aptly named "F.R.P.," and with him went the T-head four. Mercer's new-for-1915 models featured a more conventional L-head four-cylinder that, though more powerful at 70 horses, had to move a heavier, much-less-crude Raceabout around. Competition success continued in 1915 and 1916, Mercer's ride turned rapidly downhill from there.

Ferdie Roebling died in 1917, followed by his brother Charles the next year. In 1919, the Roebling family sold the company to a Wall Street investment group that brought in former Packard man Emlen Hare to run things. Hare's brainy scheme involved merging Mercer, Locomobile, and Simplex into a conglomerate called, appropriately enough, Hare Motors. But this ambitious plan quickly flopped, and Mercer was reorganized in 1921 by a group that included John Kuser. Another reorganization followed in 1924, and the firm was sold again in 1928, this time to former Chevrolet executive Harry Wahl. Wahl managed only to build one car and one display chassis before his company was swallowed up by the Great Depression. And that was that.

The mighty Mercer Raceabout's career was short but rich, if only in racing glory. Only about 550 T-head Raceabouts were built, yet each was more than capable of taking home a championship cup if so desired.

When Mercer won a race, it did so with the same car any customer could've driven. And by staying out in front at the track, the New Jersey firm demonstrated its ongoing desire to build better-performing automobiles. As the company's 1917 brochure stated, "The many lessons learned in our extensive racing experiments regarding efficiency and durability are embodied in the various Mercer models which are offered to the public. The buyer is thus assured the greatest margin of safety and reliability."

Translated: racing improves the breed.

Conventional L-head power came standard with the Model 22-70 Raceabout in 1915. Output was 70 horsepower, thus the last numeral in the name. The model code became 22-72 in 1916 and 22-73 in 1917.

Mercer introduced a more civilized two-seat roadster in 1915. Shown here is a 1917 Model 22-73 Raceabout.

The 1915 Cadillac V-8 consisted of two individually cast cylinder banks bolted to a central crankcase in a 90-degree V. Displacement was 314 cubic inches; output was 70 horsepower.

CHAPTER 3

Launching a Luxury Liner: 1915 Cadillac V-8

Size certainly did matter during the internal combustion engine's earliest days. Making more power required making more engine, first by multiplying cylinders, then by increasing displacement within those bores. One- and two-cylinder pioneering powerplants quickly gave way to the pervasive inline four-cylinder, and some of these grew to enormous proportions during the ongoing pursuit of more strength and speed.

1915 CADILLAC V-8

Type: water-cooled 90-degree V-8 L-head with electric self-starting

Construction: cast iron, two separate blocks of four cylinders each (with integral cylinder heads) bolted to common crankcase; cylinders directly opposed from each other, not staggered (detachable cylinder heads introduced in 1918)

Lubrication: pressure and splash

Main bearings: three with single-plane crankshaft and fork-and-blade connecting rods

Bore and stroke: 3.125x5.125 inches

Displacement: 314 cubic inches

Valves: in block, two per cylinder, made of tungsten steel

Camshaft: single with eight lobes, located above crankshaft in valley between cylinder banks

Compression: 4.15:1

Induction: Cadillac-produced single-throat updraft carburetor

Ignition: Delco coil-type

Horsepower: 70 at 2,400 rpm

When Henry Ford went racing in 1902 with his famed "999" machine, it was driven by a whale of a four-holer displacing 1,156 cubic inches.

It was a similar story in the regular-production world. Big cars needed big engines, and it wasn't long before the four-cylinder ran in its course as far as this country's larger, more expensive models were concerned. America's escalating luxury ranks included the "three Ps," each firing up a six-cylinder in succession—Pierce-Arrow first in 1907, Peerless later that year, followed by Packard in 1912. Cadillac, at the time well down the pricing pecking order, had introduced its first four-cylinder in 1905 and stuck with it for almost 10 years, choosing not to venture into the big-six arena.

Cadillac founder Henry Leland didn't like the inline six for various reasons, not the least of which involved the recognized tendency for that lengthy crankshaft to whip at high speeds. But he found his hand forced, as more and more customers began choosing competing sixes over his four. After building nearly 17,300 cars in 1913, Cadillac rolled out a disappointing 7,800 the following year.

Fortunately, the legend who later also founded Lincoln was no dummy. He'd already put his engineers to work on a new power source to lead the company toward a brighter, more luxurious future. Like his rivals, Leland wanted more motor, but he also wanted a more compact design that fit easily between cowl and radiator, something the long, skinny sixes didn't do well at all. What he wanted was a V-8.

Announced in September 1914, Cadillac's ground-breaking V-8 was by no means the world's first. The roots of the V layout itself run as far back as the 1860s, when steam engines began appearing in this configuration. "One supposes that the inherent virtues of compactness and excellent static and dynamic balance inspired the choice of this not necessarily obvious architecture, long before there was an automotive field in which it might manifest itself," explained noted historian Griffith Borgeson in *Automobile Quarterly* in reference to these water-fed forerunners. Gas-powered two- and four-cylinder V-type automotive engines date back almost as far as the horseless carriage itself.

As for the familiar bent eight, Frenchman Clement Ader commonly gets credit for its first automotive application, coming in three competition vehicles that ran in the Paris–Madrid race in 1903. The world's first V-8-powered regular-production automobile also came from France, in 1910, courtesy of de Dion-Bouton. American pioneers include Indianapolis' Howard Marmon, who, in 1902, assembled an experimental V-2 that reportedly used pushrod-activated overhead valves, making it one of the earliest known OHV attempts. Four years later, Marmon built a prototype 90-degree V-8 that, like his earlier two-cylinder, was air cooled.

Cylinder heads were cast integrally with each bank of four cylinders, and round inspection plates were incorporated directly above each bore. Smaller round removable plates appeared above each valve, with one of these serving as a spark plug mount.

Experiments aside, it was Cadillac that introduced America to its first successful V-8—so successful that the model it debuted in, the 1915 Type 51, became the world's first high-volume, high-priced automobile, inspiring the comment later that Leland "did for the rich what Ford had done for the poor." In December 1915, *The Automobile* claimed that the V-8 Cadillac had "ushered in a new epoch."

Cadillac built 13,000 Type 51s that first year, followed by 18,000 updated Type 53s in 1916. That same year, Peerless introduced a V-8, but typically sold about 5,000 of these annually—and that was the closest any rival would get during the V-8 Cadillac's early days. Other companies tried to follow in Cadillac's tire tracks, though most were nowhere near as successful as Peerless. Within four years of the Type 51's introduction, there were at least 22 V-8s offered in America. By 1921, however, only seven of those were still running. From 1915 to 1930, Cadillac staked its world-class reputation on nothing but V-8s.

Leland first began thinking about a V-8 in 1912. Soon afterward, Delco's Charles Kettering—the engineering genius who had supplied Cadillac with another milestone, the industry's first self-starter, late in 1911—put together a prototype V-8 for Leland after thoroughly inspecting a de Dion engine. In-house development followed in 1913, and the boss brought D. McCall White (formerly of Daimler and Napier) over from Great Britain the following year to oversee the rush to production, which was accomplished in supreme secrecy. Historians to this day question White's appointment, as well as his credentials. Nonetheless, the job got done, and in short order to boot.

White's group stuck with a basic L-head design, more or less because its valvetrain worked quieter than any other layout then in operation. Some 60 pounds lighter than the 365-cubic-inch inline four it replaced, the Type 51 engine featured two individually cast cylinder banks bolted to a central crankcase in a 90-degree V. Each bank of four cylinders incorporated an integrally

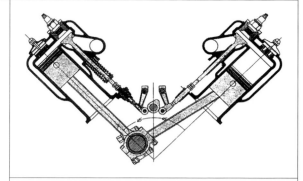

Cadillac's milestone V-8 was of conventional L-head design with valves located beside the cylinders, as opposed to overhead. Notice the roller-tipped pivoting arms between the camshaft and tappets; these pivots did away with unwanted side loading on the lifters as the cam lobe rotated by.

Each individual cylinder bank incorporated a water jacket inspection plate at both ends. The rear plate on the driver-side bank can be seen here just above the lower end of the steering column.

Cadillac offered nine V-8-powered models in 1915, including this Type 51 four-passenger salon, priced at $1,975.

A three-speed sliding-gear transmission backed up the Type 51 V-8 in 1915. *Steve and Pattie Constable photo, courtesy of General Motors*

cast cylinder head that featured a large, round, removable inspection plate directly above each bore. Smaller round plates (also removable) were located above each valve; the one topping the intake valve also served as a mount for that cylinder's spark plug. An owner (or his mechanic) could inspect either cylinder banks' water jacket by removing another pair of plates bolted on at each end of the bank.

Those banks were not staggered; rather, the four bores on one side were directly opposite the four on the other. This layout meant that combustion thrust was equal side to side, and it also translated into a shorter engine with a shorter, sturdier crankshaft and a shorter cam—all among Leland's mandates. On the other hand, putting the banks in direct opposition mandated the use of a somewhat-complicated, certainly costly "fork and blade" connecting rod design, which allowed opposing rods to dovetail together (the blade end on one side fit into the fork on the other) at their crankshaft journal mounting point.

When the Peerless V-8 appeared in 1916, it featured the now-familiar staggered-cylinder arrangement that quickly became the industry standard for V-type engines. Offsetting the cylinders meant the connecting rods could bolt side by side to the crank's journals, a layout that proved far easier and cheaper to engineer and manufacture. Cadillac, however, didn't relocate its cylinders until 1928, and Henry Leland liked the early design so much that he continued using it after opening Lincoln for business in 1920. Lincoln's classic KB, introduced in 1932, still relied on fork-and-blade rods inside its smooth-running V-12.

Cadillac's Type 51 V-8 was made up essentially of two four-cylinder engines together on a shared crankcase. The V-8 retained the inline four's 180-degree, single-plane (translated, all throws were directly opposed) crankshaft, which was held in place by three main bearings.

And just as it did inside the old four, the 180-degree crank tended to shake the V-8 horizontally as the two banks fought each other. Little fuss was made over this inherent vibration when the Cadillac V-8 first made the scene, but Cadillac finally addressed the hassle in 1924 by installing a modern 90-degree, two-plane crank, making the Type 63's new engine the industry's first truly balanced V-8.

Bore and stroke for the Type 51 V-8 measured 3.125 and 5.125 inches, respectively, bringing displacement to 314 cubic inches. Maximum output was 70 horsepower at 2,400 rpm. Compression was 4.15:1. Two shaft-driven water pumps, located down low at the crankshaft's nose, cooled the engine, and this system featured yet another innovation pioneered by Cadillac, thermostatic control.

The cross shaft that spun the water pumps' impellers also operated the oil pump, which sent lubricant from the reservoir below through a pipe inside the crankcase to the crankshaft's main bearings. Passages drilled into the crank allowed pressurized oil to flow to the rod bearings. Additional piping allowed more oil to reach the camshaft bearings. The pistons and cylinder walls were lubricated by a simple splash method, as overflow oil was thrown from the rods.

The cam incorporated eight lobes, as opposing valves each shared one. Made of tungsten steel, the exhaust valves were typical flat-faced pieces, while their intake counterparts were tulip-shaped to "facilitate the intake of the gas." And though the valves weren't overhead, the Type 51 engine featured rocker arms, which engaged the cam's lobes through roller tips and rocked on pivots to activate the pushrod's tappets without transferring any side loading.

A single-throat updraft carburetor fed the Type 51 V-8 through generous intake tubing that ran below the large exhaust manifolds that dominated the top view of the engine. These manifolds ran back and down the rear of each cylinder bank and fed dual tailpipes and mufflers. Delco's superior coil ignition system supplied the spark, and the Delco-supplied starter motor served double duty as a generator for the car's electricals. Along with self-starting, Cadillac was an industry pioneer in battery ignition and electric lighting. Most rivals were still using magnetos at the time.

The Type 51 engine represented a real mover and shaker in 1915. "Of the Cadillac 8's behavior on the road, it would be difficult to speak too highly," claimed a *Country Life* report. "The engine's acceleration has to be experienced to be believed."

Performance got a boost in 1916, when Cadillac fitted the Type 53 V-8 with an enlarged intake manifold that helped boost output to 77 horsepower. To demonstrate this newfound strength, Cannonball Baker and W. F. Sturm took a V-8 roadster cross-country in May 1916, traveling 3,714 miles in seven days, 11 hours, and 52 minutes. This time was some four days faster than the previous transcontinental record, set by a Stutz Bearcat. Further upgrades included detachable cylinder heads for the 1918 Type 57 V-8.

A dozen years later, Cadillac made big-time headlines again, that time with twice as many cylinders. But that's another story, for another chapter.

The Cadillac V-8 was boosted to 77 horsepower in 1916. Shown here is the 1917 Type 55 V-8, which still displaced 314 cubic inches.

Detachable cylinder heads debuted for Cadillac's Type 57 V-8 in 1918.

Called the "Cast-Iron Wonder" when it first appeared in 1929, Chevrolet's overhead-valve six-cylinder became the first Corvette's heart and soul in 1953. Three side-draft carburetors helped the Corvette six produce 150 horsepower that year, then 155 in 1954. Displacement was 235 cubic inches.

CHAPTER 4

From Stovebolt to Sporting Life:
Chevrolet Blue Flame Six-Cylinder

Not all great American cars have been home to great American engines.

Consider the Corvette, which in 2003 celebrated its 50th birthday. We take this

sporting proposition for granted today, knowing

full well that within those plastic confines reside

some of the most magnificent mechanicals

presently available from Detroit.

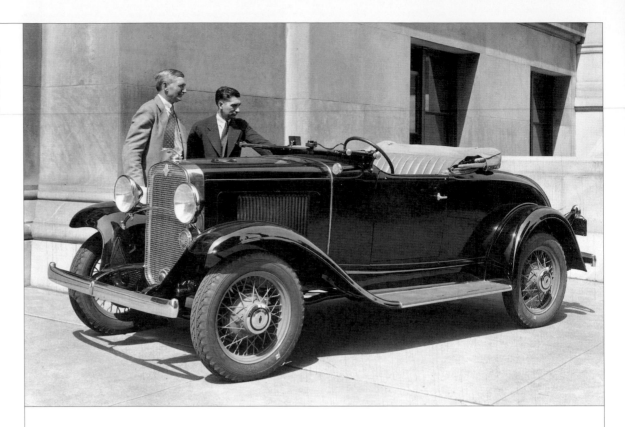

Former Ford man William Knudsen (at left) became Chevrolet president and general manager in 1924 and then directed Chevy into the number one sales spot three years later. Here, Knudsen and Division Vice President H. J. Klingler admire a 1931 six-cylinder roadster.

Both the C6 (sixth-generation) Corvette as a whole and its LS2 V-8 heart deserve honored resting places in automotive Valhalla once their days in this world are done. But the jury wasn't so willing to hand down a guilty verdict when the question of the Corvette's classic nature was first addressed a half century ago. All early fiberglass-bodied two-seaters built in 1953 and 1954 were powered by the only engine Chevrolet offered in those days: a rather mundane inline six-cylinder. Though noticeably warmed over, the "Blue Flame" six was still just a six, a plain fact not missed by V-8-crazed Yankees who simply couldn't warm up to America's first modern sports car. Not until its own V-8 showed up in 1955 did the Corvette truly take off, both literally and figuratively.

That's not to say, however, that Chevrolet's long-standing six-cylinder didn't have its own day in the sun. Originally called the "Cast-Iron Wonder," the earliest rendition of this engine made major headlines when introduced in 1929 and continued running strong from there, through various updates (some minor, a couple major), as the driving force behind what was America's best-selling automobile for nearly every year after 1930. So dramatic was the Cast-Iron Wonder's debut that it even forced Henry Ford—who up until 1927 had known nothing but first place in Detroit's sales race for 20 years—to trade his beloved four cylinders in on a new V-8, resulting in even bolder headlines. But as much of a milestone as Henry's "flathead" V-8 was, it still couldn't overtake Chevy's "Stovebolt" six over the long haul. While Ford did temporarily rise back up to the head of the sales pack in 1935, it was Chevrolet that dominated from then on. The Bowtie band was still riding high behind its "U.S. 1" banner 20 years later, when Chevy's own V-8 finally emerged to steal the show from the old, reliable Stovebolt.

First opened for business in November 1911 by General Motors founder William Durant, the Chevrolet Motor Company originally relied on a T-head six-cylinder engine to get things rolling and turned to a highly successful overhead-valve four-cylinder in 1913. An L-head six did appear in 1915, as did an OHV V-8 in 1917, but neither of these engines proved viable, leaving the OHV four to power Chevrolet on its drive to the top.

Ford's Tin Lizzie was Billy Durant's target all along, though the famous racer his company was named for wholeheartedly disagreed. From the moment Durant had hired him, Louis Chevrolet had envisioned his moniker emblazoned on the noses of higher-priced, high-performance automobiles. But the boss won out, and Chevrolet quit in disgust in September 1913, leaving his contractually bound surname behind. Bowtie popularity soared from there, and Chevrolet was selling more than 125,000 cars a year by 1917. The company then joined the GM fraternity in May 1918.

The rest is history, as was Billy Durant within a few short years. After GM stock nose-dived in 1920, angry stockholders forced a corporate reorganization resulting in Durant's banishment, his second in 10 years. This time, he didn't make a comeback, at least not with the giant conglomerate he had helped build. He founded another (albeit much smaller) automotive empire, but it was knocked down by the Depression in 1932. Then, like Louis Chevrolet, Billy Durant fell into obscurity. The former died in 1941, the latter six years later.

Chevrolet nearly expired as well not long after Durant's ousting. GM's new leadership considered killing the low-priced car, but Alfred Sloan Jr. would have none of it. Sloan, the big man brought in to sort through the mess left behind by Durant, argued against ending the burgeoning Bowtie bloodline. He suggested redirecting the division toward a more promising future, a place where Chevrolet didn't have to necessarily butt heads directly with Ford yet still could exist as an equal. Or better. A new niche was created where the Chevy cost a little more than its rival from Dearborn, but those extra dollars bought a little more refinement, a little more comfort, a little more car.

All that, combined with the emergence of former Ford production manager William S. Knudsen as the division's new president and general manager in 1924, helped Chevrolet set a new course toward not only meeting but actually unseating Ford atop Detroit's sales leader board. That year, Ford sold eight vehicles for every one Chevy. In 1925, that ratio dropped to 4:1. In 1926, it was less than 3:1. Chevrolet became *numero uno* for the first time in 1927, though it must be said that Henry Ford contributed at least partially to this achievement by shutting down his company temporarily that year in order to reorganize production lines for his highly anticipated Model A. Chevy topped the charts again, by far, in 1928, but Ford retook the lead the next year after the Model A got warmed up. A truly tough battle ensued as Chevrolet by then had its own new model up and running.

A December 1928 *Automobile Trade Journal* report called it "an epoch in motor car development." Company promotional paperwork designated it "the outstanding Chevrolet of Chevrolet history." Introduced just before Thanksgiving 1928, the object of all this acclaim was

---

1954 CHEVROLET CORVETTE

Type: water-cooled OHV inline six-cylinder

Construction: cast-iron block and cylinder head

Lubrication: fully pressurized

Main bearings: four

Bore and stroke: 3.56x3.93 inches

Displacement: 235 cubic inches

Valves: overhead, mounted on common rocker shaft, two per cylinder, dual springs

Camshaft: single with solid lifters

Compression: 8:1

Induction: three Carter single-throat side-draft carburetors

Ignition: coil and breaker points

Exhaust: split manifold, dual mufflers and tailpipes

Horsepower: 155 at 4,200 rpm

the division's new six-cylinder engine, a smooth, efficient overhead-valve powerplant that picked up where Chevy's tried-and-true four-cylinder left off. Although various initial prototypes built prior to February 1927 all had been of the yeoman L-head design, a more advanced OHV six represented the logical step up. After all, the well-worn company slogan had always been "valves in head, ahead in value."

Value remained a merit of Chevrolet's new engine, so much so that a new slogan was also in order: "six in the price range of a four." Bottom lines for various 1929 six-cylinder models ranged only $10 to $30 higher compared to their four-cylinder forerunners from 1928. And those extra bucks not only bought two additional cylinders, they also paid for 23 more cubic inches and 11 more horses. Rated at 46 horsepower, the 194-ci six was fed by a Carter one-barrel mounted in the then-typical updraft position. Bore and stroke measured 3.3125 by 3.75 inches.

Not so typical was the crank, which was called "a new development in the manufacture of six-cylinder crankshafts." Weighing 46 pounds, it consisted of a single-plane forging that was balanced both statically and dynamically. Unfortunately, it was only held in place by three main bearings, and it also handled the bulk of the lubrication chores by the age-old splash method. A less-than-stout bottom end represented the original Stovebolt's primary weakness.

That nickname resulted from the engine's various 1/4-inch slot-head bolts, cheap-looking choices that helped keep costs down. Cost-conscious iron also was used to cast the pistons, leading some wag somewhere to blurt out "Cast-Iron Wonder," commentary that, like the Stovebolt moniker, at first constituted a slap at Chevrolet's tightwad approach. Company officials liked neither tag, but both hung around for quite a while, and Stovebolt later even became an affectionate reference that, in some minds, stood for the engine's simple, durable, no-nonsense nature.

Whatever the name, the Chevy six was a real winner, a plain fact Henry Ford quickly discovered. William Knudsen had first ordered his engineers to create the Cast-Iron Wonder after he learned that Ford had a new model in the works. Tit for tat. The new six was even ready for 1928, but Knudsen chose to hold back and let the Model A have the limelight first. Meanwhile, his designers added four more inches to the wheelbases of Chevrolet's revamped National-series cars and trucks for 1928. A *MoTor* review of the National line explained it was "interesting to note" that every one of those inches had been added at the vehicles' noses—to make room for two extra cylinders perhaps?

Knudsen rolled out his new Chevrolet six about a year after Ford's four-cylinder Model A first made headlines. Although the A had its way in 1929 and 1930, it was the Stovebolt Chevy that reigned supreme in 1931 and again in 1932, even after Henry Ford had made more history by introducing his flathead V-8.

Improvements along the way included a slight output jump, to 50 horsepower, for 1930. That figure rose again to 60 horsepower in 1932 thanks to a compression increase, more valve lift, and a new intake mounting a Carter downdraft carburetor. The cylinder block also was recast that year for extra strength, and pressure lubrication was instituted for the cam and crank's

Chevrolet boosted six-cylinder displacement from 216 cubic inches to 235 for truck applications in 1947. Shown here is a 1950 truck engine, which also appeared that year for Chevy passenger cars fitted with the division's new Powerglide automatic transmission. *Steve and Pattie Constable photo, courtesy of General Motors*

All 300 Corvettes built for 1953 featured six-cylinder power and Powerglide automatic transmissions, and all were painted Polo White. No exterior door handles were used, nor was roll-up side glass. Eurostyle side curtains were standard.

main bearings. Displacement then rose—and dropped—in 1933 as two six-cylinders were offered, one at 206 cubic inches, the other at 181. The 65-horse 206-ci six was created by stroking the Stovebolt (to 4.00 inches), while de-stroking it (to 3.5 inches) produced the 181-ci engine, which was discontinued after 1935.

A marked increase to 80 horsepower for the newly named "Blue Streak" six allowed promotional people to guarantee 80 miles per hour for the 1934 Chevrolet. Reportedly, engineers produced those extra horses by tweaking the combustion chambers, and this perhaps explains why the name was changed to "Blue Flame" in 1935. Brochures later used the term "blue flame" to describe the superior combustion process made possible by the Chevy six's cylinder head design.

A major redesign was performed for 1937 with the focus being to increase durability along with power potential. The cylinder block was recast with extra length, while deck height was shortened by 2 inches. The latter change went hand in hand with a rev-conscious shortened stroke, while the stretched block made extra room for both bigger bores and a switch from three main bearings to four. Even though the stroke was shortened from 4.0 to 3.75 inches, displacement increased to 216.5 cubic inches thanks to those bigger 3.5-inch bores. Output was 85 horsepower.

Yet another displacement increase occurred in 1950, after Chevrolet introduced its first (also the low-priced field's first) automatic transmission, Powerglide. Like most early automatics, the slip-sliding Powerglide needed extra muscle to operate as designed, so Chevy officials borrowed the big 235-ci six, used in heavy trucks since 1947, for this automotive application. With a bore and stroke of 3.5625 by 3.9375 inches, the 235-cubic-inch six was advertised at 105 horsepower and also was the first engine in the low-priced ranks with hydraulic lifters. Manual-transmission cars continued using the solid-lifter, 216.5-cubic-inch six, rated at 92 horsepower.

This same dual-purpose lineup carried over through 1952, the year Ford unveiled a new 101-horsepower, 215-ci six-cylinder that *Motor Trend* called "the engine that can, and will, go places in the years ahead." In comparison, another critic at the time claimed the old Stovebolt was "as up-to-date as red flannel underwear." Apparently figuring that those undies needed changing, Chevy engineers modernized the Powerglide six for 1953, perhaps most importantly by graduating it to full-pressure lubrication. Insert-type connecting rod bearings also were added, and those trademark cast-iron pistons were exchanged for lightweight aluminum slugs, effectively ending the Cast-Iron Wonder era. With a compression increase from 6.7:1 to 7.5:1, the 1953 automatic-trans six produced 115 horsepower, and it was this engine that served as a base for the original Corvette's heart and soul.

Debuting at New York's Waldorf-Astoria hotel in January 1953, the first Corvette came only with a Powerglide-backed 235-ci Blue Flame six, though that wasn't as bad as it sounded, certainly not for the time. Sure, the automatic-only situation was tough to stomach, especially by American car buyers who knew by then that all real sports cars came with a stick. But at 150

Corvette engines in 1953 breathed through three crude bullet inlets; early in 1954 these were replaced by two conventional air cleaners.

horsepower, the modified Blue Flame engine was able to blast one of those Polo White two-seaters all the way up to 110 miles per hour, and from rest to 60 miles per hour in 11 seconds, both laudable achievements for 1953. As *Motor Life's* Hank Gamble saw it, "The Corvette is a beauty—and it *goes!*"

Various modifications helped transform the venerable Stovebolt into the Corvette's Blue Flame six. For starters, compression was boosted up to 8:1 and a more aggressive solid-lifter cam was stuffed inside. Lift was 0.405 inch on intake, 0.414 on exhaust. A metal cam gear replaced the stock fiber piece, all the better to let this inline six rev beyond 5,000 rpm with confidence. Valvetrain gear also was beefed with dual valve springs and stronger exhaust valves.

Three Carter one-barrel carburetors, mounted in side-draft fashion to clear the Corvette's low, forward-hinged hood, were bolted onto a special aluminum intake manifold. Although three round air cleaners were used in prototype applications, these were replaced in production by a trio of small air inlet extensions. Exhaust chores, meanwhile, were handled by a split manifold that dumped into dual pipes and mufflers.

Additional special touches included a high-efficiency water pump and shielding for the distributor and plug wires—the latter added to prevent ignition voltage from wrecking havoc with radio reception. Remember, fiberglass panels don't suppress this interference like typical steel bodies do. As for the high-volume water pump, it was relocated low on the front of the Corvette engine to again allow more hood clearance, in this case for the accompanying four-bladed fan.

Also mounted low for obvious reasons, the Blue Flame six's radiator required a remote header tank, which, on the Waldorf-Astoria prototype, was located on the driver's side of the valve cover, running parallel with the engine. In production, this tank was switched to the opposite side. Yet another change made while transforming the show car into a street machine involved the carbs—the prototype's automatic choke was exchanged for a cable-operated manual setup in production.

Only 300 Corvettes were built that first year, followed by 3,640 more in 1954, all fitted with Blue Flame six-cylinders and Powerglide automatics. Running changes made during 1954 included a new cam (that boosted output to 155 horsepower) and a more functional induction setup that replaced those three bullet-shaped inlets for two round air cleaners mounted conventionally in upright fashion. Longer exhaust tips in back (added to help prevent spent gases from staining the paint on the car's tail) also appeared very early in the 1954 Corvette run.

Corvette production for 1955 was only 700, with seven of those featuring the Blue Flame six. Fortunately, the other 693 were powered that year by Chevrolet's hot, high-winding 265-ci V-8, which produced 195 truly appreciated horses when dropped between fiberglass flanks. Talk about a transformation.

As for Chevrolet's Stovebolt, it continued soldiering on after being pulled from the Corvette lineup, surviving into the early 1960s before finally retiring, quite honorably. It might not have been necessarily a great engine, but it did a great job for a great many years.

A split exhaust manifold allowed the Corvette's Blue Flame six-cylinder to exhale spent gases through less-restrictive dual pipes and mufflers. All other six-cylinder Chevys used single exhausts.

Ford's first flathead V-8 displaced 221 cubic inches and featured cast-iron cylinder heads. Output in 1932 was 65 horsepower. Twenty-one studs held down each cylinder head; improved 24-stud heads appeared in 1939.

CHAPTER 5

Twice Four Is More: Ford Flathead V-8

Dearborn's first V-8, introduced in 1932, also was Detroit's first mass-

produced, low-priced eight, with an emphasis on mass-produced. Arch

rival Chevrolet technically was first in the field

with a V-8, introducing an overhead-valve variety

in 1917, but sold only about 2,700 examples

before thankfully giving up the ill-fated venture

after a year or so.

1932 FORD MODEL 18

Type: water-cooled 90-degree V-8 L-head with electric self-starting

Construction: cast-iron monobloc with detachable cylinder heads (held down by 21 nuts and studs, increased to 24 studs in 1939)

Lubrication: fully pressurized

Main bearings: three with forged-steel counterweighted crankshaft

Bore and stroke: 3.0625x3.75 inches

Displacement: 221 cubic inches

Valves: in block, two per cylinder, made of high-chrome silicon alloy steel, 1.537-inch diameter

Camshaft: single with solid lifters

Compression: 5.5:1

Induction: Detroit Lubricator single-throat downdraft carburetor on aluminum intake manifold

Exhaust: single muffler and tailpipe

Ignition: coil and breaker points

Horsepower: 65 at 3,400 rpm

At about $1,500, Chevy's V-8-powered Model D didn't exactly qualify as "low-priced," and it was that uncharacteristically high (for General Motors' price leader) bottom line that guaranteed failure from the start. Ford's little "flathead" V-8, on the other hand, cost about a third of that 15 years later, a plain fact that the common man simply couldn't miss. As ol' Henry himself later explained, "We did not invent the eight-cylinder car. What we did was make it possible for the average family to own one."

Simple, affordable, even lovable, the flathead V-8 managed to survive for nearly a quarter-century in an ever-changing market, this despite various inherent weaknesses that seemingly endeared this sometimes problem-plagued powerplant even more to its faithful owners. Gremlins came along for the ride in force early on, primarily thanks to the mad rush in bringing this milestone to market. While fixes were performed immediately in 1932, and various improvements appeared as the years passed, some pesky problems managed to hang on almost unchecked. Flatheads were always prone to use oil, and overheating was all too common, the latter thanks to exhaust passages cast through the water jackets within the cylinder block and the poor location of the twin water pumps on early engines. Equally poor initial mounting points for both the fuel pump and distributor also helped induce maladies. Excessive engine heat would cook the fuel in the pump, creating vapor lock. Power outages were common, as the distributor was originally attached down low in front where invading water could easily short it out.

But once initial teething troubles were dealt with, there was no stopping Henry's "eight for the price of a four." His flathead rolled on up through 1953, then continued running strong as a popular hot rodders' toy for almost another decade before finally fading from the limelight, but not completely away. Even today, there exists a diehard faction among the wrench-bending set who remain true blue to this meat-and-potatoes mill. "Flatheads forever" is their motto.

Henry Ford (at right) with the crude *999* race car that first brought him fame in 1901. At the controls is legendary driver Barney Oldfield. Powering the *999* machine was a huge four-cylinder that displaced more than 1,100 cubic inches.

Explaining the "flathead" nickname is easy enough, considering that this pioneering V-8 wore cylinder heads that were nothing more than thin, flat covers with combustion areas carved out of their undersides. Like its forerunner, the Model T four-cylinder, and all other L-heads, Ford's first V-8 kept its valves facing upward within its cylinder block, an uncomplicated layout that stayed in step with Henry's ever-present demands for practical simplicity.

His flathead V-8 was certainly simple, almost to a fault. Save for its innovative one-piece cylinder block, it represented no great shakes as far as engineering advancement was concerned. In fact, it looked very much like a dinosaur from the start—certainly so after World War II when General Motors began rolling out its thoroughly modern short-stroke, overhead-valve V-8s. The compact V layout itself was nothing new by 1932, and one-piece monobloc V-8s also had appeared before, as early as 1916, though in very limited numbers. Most prominent were those introduced by GM engineers in 1929 for Oldsmobile's short-lived Viking and the Pontiac/ Oakland tag team.

It was left up to Ford engineers, however, to develop entirely new processes to efficiently cast and machine lightweight one-piece cylinder blocks, an achievement that was the key to keeping costs low and production high. Manufacturing all previous monoblocs had represented a highly expensive proposition, and this precluded any mass-production ventures into Detroit's low-priced ranks. Ford's monobloc milepost, contrarily, was amazingly cheap to build, and in unprecedented numbers to boot. The boss initially demanded that his River Rouge foundry produce a whopping 3,000 V-8 cylinder blocks a day, and he wasn't disappointed. At best, Oldsmobile was turning out 4,000 or 5,000 of its monobloc V-8s—in a year.

Although demand was a little slow catching up to those sky-high supply rates in 1932, sales did soar once the early glitches were addressed. Ford's flathead eventually attracted buyers by the millions—12 to be semiexact—from 1932 to 1953. Included in this crowd were two satisfied customers who attracted devoted followings of their own. Chicago gangster John Dillinger and fellow bad guy Clyde Barrow relied on V-8 Fords for more than one harrowing escape from the law. As legend has it, Dillinger and Barrow each wrote Henry Ford personally to extol the merits of his hot little V-8. In the words of the former, written on May 16, 1934, "You have a wonderful car." Continued Dillinger, "Your slogan should be: 'Drive a Ford and watch the other cars fall behind you.' I can make any other car take a Ford's dust!"

While Bonnie and Clyde often failed to pay for the cars they drove, typical Ford customers had to. No problem. Prices for a '32 V-8 Ford began at $460 for a two-door roadster—only $50 more than its four-cylinder counterpart. V-8 power—65 advertised horses in the first flathead's case—had never before come this cheap. Nor had it ever come in such a compact package, making the flathead Ford an instant hit among the competition crowd.

Offering decent power potential in a reasonably light chassis, early V-8 Fords were soon dominating sanctioned stock-car racing, and continued doing so as late as 1948—much later at less professional levels. Ford V-8s also appeared at Indianapolis in the 1930s, courtesy of, among others, Henry Miller and Preston Tucker. Britain Sydney Allard too turned to Ford power for his

Henry Ford made automotive history again in 1932 when he offered affordable V-8 power to the masses for the first time.

Ford introduced an economy-conscious flathead in 1937, the so-called V8-60, named for its output rating of 60 horsepower. This tiny 136-cubic-inch weakling (at left, beside a 1932 221-ci V-8) survived only through 1940.

hybrid racers in 1936 and was still using flatheads in his impressive J2 roadsters in 1950. An employee of Allard's, Zora Arkus-Duntov, first made a name for himself in America by creating the legendary Ardun overhead-valve conversion for Ford's flathead in 1947, before joining GM's Corvette engineer team six years later.

Along with all these big names, came hoards of lesser-known hot rodders, all attracted to the flattie by its availability. Junkyards were full of this cheap power source by the late 1940s, and from there its hot rod potential grew, as aftermarket performance parts became more plentiful through the 1950s. Even though it quickly lost ground with the jet set after Chevrolet introduced its own milestone V-8 in 1955, the venerable flathead could still be found winning at drag strips and turning heads at malt shops into the 1960s. So what if southern California's Beach Boys first made the hit parade by singing the praises of Chevy's fabled 409 V-8? They also were known to croon over their little "Deuce" coupe with its "ported and relieved, stroked and bored" flathead able to thrash "a Thunderbird like it's standing still."

Flathead roots date back to 1921, when Ford secretly began experimenting on larger engines to someday supersede its tried-and-true four-banger. The Model T's replacement was not far from the drawing boards at the time, and Henry Ford apparently had hoped that his new model would debut with more cylinders up front. But engine design work hadn't progressed nearly far enough in time for the Model A's 1928 debut, so the old four continued soldiering on alone. Then along came Chevrolet's overhead-valve six the following year, forcing the boss' hand. Merely matching the Stovebolt's challenge, however, wouldn't do. As he had already told engineer Fred Thoms a few years before, "We're going to go from a four to an eight, because Chevrolet is going to a six."

Knowing that Chevy's six was on the way, Henry Ford, in 1928, put more than one engineering team hard at work developing a V-8. Yet another design project was kicked off in November 1930, this one headed by Carl Schultz under strict direction of Henry Ford himself. Schultz's group worked under such secrecy that not even chief engineer Laurence Sheldrick was aware of their efforts early on, and by February 1931, they had a test engine up and running after prototype cylinder blocks had been hand-cast at River Rouge. Prototype V-8 installations in Model A chassis began the next spring, followed by the official decision to go into full production in December.

Designing and testing prototypes was one thing. But putting that design into mass production at a cost compatible with Henry Ford's ideals represented a whole 'nother ball of wax, especially since no one before had even considered mass-producing a monobloc V-8. What made Ford people think they could do it? For one thing, they had Charles "Cast-Iron Charlie" Sorensen on their side.

Sorensen, who was Ford's production boss, had hooked up with the company in 1905 as a patternmaker, and had played a major role in making the Model T's assembly line work. By 1931, it was again up to him to help make history by creating yet another well-oiled machine. Critics up to that point still claimed a mass-produced monobloc couldn't be done, but Ford men knew better. As Laurence Sheldrick remembered, "Sorensen, with his magic in the pattern shops and foundries, assured us it could be done, and it was. He actually had a pilot line ready before the announcement came on production. Between January and March, this thing was whipped into shape."

"We studied every move in the molding operation and mechanized its handling," recalled Sorenson later in his book, *My Forty Years with Ford*. Keys to the operation included proximity of the processes and continuous movement. Once finished, the molds were hoisted onto a conveyer, where they met another conveyer full of the various cores fresh from their nearby ovens. From there, the completed molds, each stuffed with 43 cores, conveyed on at an unheard of rate of 100 per hour through the iron pouring line. Meanwhile, a 2-ton overhead pouring furnace—fed by a nearby 20-ton electric furnace—moved right along with the conveyer, filling the molds with molten iron while still in motion.

"Achievement of a continuous moving operation of this foundry work eliminated all the back-breaking toil from the molding, pouring, and handling of the casting as it came out of the mold," added Sorensen. "It was a revolutionary method, developed entirely within the Ford organization. There was nothing like it anywhere else on a comparable scale."

All told, Henry Ford spent $50 million to upgrade the Rouge foundry for the V-8 casting process. And taking lessons they learned creating the flathead's one-piece block, Sorensen's men next pioneered the cast-steel crankshaft, which replaced their much-more-expensive-to-manufacture forged crank in 1934. Two years later, *Automotive Industries* would call Ford's cast crank "one of the most important contributions to automotive engineering in recent years."

The end result of Ford's new manufacturing processes was a 90-degree L-head V-8 with a bore of 3.0625 inches and a stroke of 3.75. Displacement came to 221 cubic inches. Topping the one-piece block were cast-iron cylinder heads held down by 21 nuts and studs. Inside were special heat-treated aluminum alloy pistons, a forged-steel 65-pound counterweighted crankshaft with three main bearings, and babbit-backed bearing surfaces. The camshaft and connecting rods were also of forged steel. Valves were of high-chrome silicon alloy steel. Valve diameter was 1.537 inches, lift was 0.292 inches. Compression was 5.5:1.

Full-pressure lubrication was supplied by a camshaft-driven gear-type pump. And two belt-driven water pumps, located at the top of each head, helped move water along through what was still basically an archaic thermosyphon system, explaining some of the inherent cooling problems. As for fuel delivery chores, a Detroit Lubricator single-throat carburetor rode atop an aluminum intake manifold that also served as a valve chamber cover. An A.C. fuel pump was mounted on the rear of the intake; the belt-driven generator was perched above up front. The integral distributor/coil assembly was mounted horizontally at the front of the engine to allow the distributor to be driven directly by the camshaft. On the exhaust end, symmetrical cast-iron exhaust manifolds were joined together by a cross-over pipe to allow spent gases to flow into a single muffler.

Ford had already introduced its updated Model B with a revamped four-cylinder when the new V-8-powered Model 18—"8" signifying the cylinder count, "1" identifying it as the company's first eight—debuted on March 31, 1932. Reportedly, 5.5 million people rushed into Ford

Unbolting the nonstock high-compression aluminum head on this modified Mercury flathead and flipping it over atop the block shows why L-heads also were called side-valve engines. Both valves were located within the block to the inside of the cylinder bores. Note the complicated combustion chamber shape in the head's underside.

showrooms that day to get their first look at what was basically a freshened Model A rolling on a longer wheelbase—106 inches compared to 103.5. Weighing only about 2,500 pounds—some 600 or 700 pounds lighter than eight-cylinder models from Pontiac, Oldsmobile, and Willys—the '32 V-8 Ford offered an exceptional power-to-weight ratio for its day. Additionally, the flathead's horsepower-per-cubic-inch measurement was tops among 16 rivals in Detroit's lower-priced ranks.

Top end for the Model 18 was 80 miles per hour, but it couldn't run away from those afore-mentioned gremlins. Of the 178,749 Model 18s sold in 1932, reportedly the first 4,250 delivered by April had to be returned to dealers for various engine repairs, most major. Nonetheless, Ford managed to survive this potentially deadly debut and save the flathead's image, first by applying band-aids, then through a series of engineering upgrades.

First came a redesigned aluminum cylinder head with reshaped combustion chambers that upped the fuel/air squeeze to 6.3:1. Maximum output, accordingly, also increased, to 75 horse-power. The aforementioned cast-alloy crankshaft was added in 1934, as was a new dual-throat carburetor, the Stromberg 48, on a redesigned dual-plane intake manifold that helped cure a rough-running problem caused by the inherent unequal fuel distribution characteristics of the previously used single-passage intake. These upgrades increased maximum horsepower yet again, this time to 85 horses. Reported top speed was now 87 miles per hour.

Dearborn introduced a second, smaller flathead V-8 in 1937, undoubtedly in response to ever-present requests for a Ford six, which had grown even more plentiful after the company's long-trusted four-cylinder engine was dropped after 1934. Offering "four-cylinder economy combined with eight-cylinder smoothness," the 136-ci V-8—with its 2.6-inch bore and 3.2-inch stroke—was brought over from the European market, where it had been motivating Brits and Frenchmen for a year.

Prices for Ford's first V-8 models in 1932 began at a tidy $460. Four-cylinder models disappeared after 1934, and in 1935 a V-8-powered roadster cost $550. Its upscale Cabriolet running mate was based at $625 that year.

Although simply a scaled-down version of its existing 221-ci cousin, the 136-ci flathead did have some unique features. Most noticeable were interchangeable aluminum heads held down by 17 studs, and a relocated oil pump. Incorporated with the front main bearing cap, this pump was driven off the crank instead of the cam. Maximum output was predictably less, 60 horsepower, while fuel economy was equally predictable—roughly 25 miles per gallon, up from the 20 to 22 cruising miles per gallon normally encountered by drivers of the larger flathead Ford.

That improved fuel economy was the main attraction for the so-called "V-8/60" Fords (the larger flathead became known as, you guessed it, the "V-8/85") in 1937. More than 300,000 were sold. But once drivers found the car could hardly get out of its own way, or even that of the earlier Model B with its four fewer cylinders, interest began to wane. The little V-8/60 was history by 1941, the year Ford finally introduced a six.

Before he started playing with Corvettes, Zora Arkus-Duntov ran the Ardun Engine Company in New York. In 1947, the Ardun firm developed an overhead-valve conversion kit for the Ford flathead V-8. Estimates claim that about 200 to 250 pairs of Ardun heads were cast for 85- and 100-horse flatheads, along with perhaps another dozen for the smaller V8-60 of 1937–1940. At right is a highly priced Ardun flathead; at left is an equally hot flattie hopped up with a Roots-type supercharger.

Meanwhile, the existing 221-ci V-8 was treated to a whole host of improvements in 1937. On top, the famed Stromberg 97 carburetor replaced the series 48. Inside, main bearing diameters went from 2 inches to 2.4 and new insert-type bearings were added. Also, new cast-steel domed pistons filled the cylinders, working in concert with redesigned aluminum heads, featuring improved combustion chambers to in turn improve squelch characteristics. This translated into better volumetric efficiency, which meant higher compression was not required to keep power levels up. Thus, the V-8/85 used 6.12:1 compression to make its 85 advertised horses. The redesigned heads also helped ease cooling problems, as the water outlets were moved to their centers and the water pumps were relocated to the front of the block, or the entrance side of the system.

The next major upgrade came in 1939, the year the upscale Mercury debuted with a bored-out flathead V-8 of its own, a 239-ci version rated at 95 horsepower. Compression for the Merc V-8 was 6.3:1, compared to 6.1:1 for the 85-horsepower 221-ci Ford flathead. The new, larger

Ford flathead V-8s helped get drag racing rolling in the early 1950s. Though soon superseded on developing drag strips by Chrysler's hemi-head V-8, the flathead remained a rodding favorite into the 1960s. And some flatties, like this Merc-powered example, were still seen racing relatively successfully at grass roots levels as late as the 1970s.

Merc engine also featured a tougher crank with 2.5-inch-diameter main journals. Both Ford and Mercury V-8s in 1939 were also treated to revised 24-stud heads for improved sealing. These heads were again modified in 1942, upping compression to 6.2:1 for Ford and 6.4:1 for Mercury. Power was then 90 horsepower for the former, 100 for the latter.

After the war, the 239-ci V-8 was used in both applications from 1946 to 1948, designated "59-A" for Ford, "59-B" for Mercury. A Holley two-barrel carburetor was added on top; compression was 6.8:1, while output remained at 100 horsepower.

The last—and by far most significant—update for the flathead V-8 came in 1949 as part of Henry Ford II and Ernest R. Breech's massive modernization effort. Breech had left General Motors' Bendix Division the previous summer to join Ford, and he'd brought various other GM men with him. Among these was Harold Youngren, who had been Oldsmobile's chief engineer for 15 years.

Youngren did his best upgrading the venerable flathead. Cooling, oil consumption, and ignition were all greatly improved. The 24-stud heads remained for 1949 but had their water outlets back up front instead of in the center. Also finally relocated, the redesigned distributor (with vacuum spark advance instead of centrifugal) went from its former wet spot down low to a higher, drier position atop the front of the engine, where it was driven by the cam through a spiral bevel gear. A separate bell housing was introduced (as opposed to the integral unit previously incorporated), as was an improved crankshaft with new nonfloating, insert-type connecting rod bearings.

The Ford crank, cast of nodular iron, still featured a 3.75-inch stroke (to go with its 3.1875-inch bore), but Mercury's new forged crank had 4-inch throws, meaning displacement was increased to 255 cubic inches. While output for the improved 239-ci Ford V-8 remained at 100 horsepower, the enlarged Mercury flathead was accordingly up-rated to 112 horses. Both still relied on 6.8:1 compression.

More cooling improvements came in 1951, this time to help make the flathead V-8 more compatible for operation in front of Ford's first automatic transmission, the Fordomatic. A final enhancement of note came the following year when flathead compression was bumped up to 7.2:1, translating into a power increase to 110 horses for Ford's 239-ci V-8 and 125 for Mercury's larger 255-ci variety.

Various other minor improvements were made in the early 1950s, but all at Ford knew it was only a matter of time before retirement finally came for what *Motor Trend* in 1952 called an "engine of the past." Dearborn's first modern overhead-valve V-8, the 239-ci "Y-block," finally appeared in 1954, signaling the end of the line for the long-running power source that *Special Interest Auto*'s Mike Lamm labeled, "Henry Ford's last mechanical triumph."

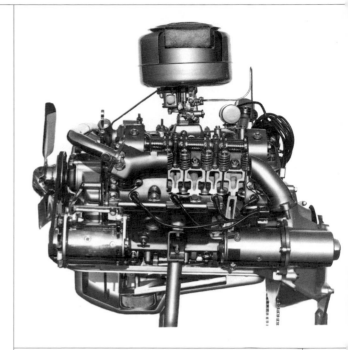

Ford finally retired the flathead in 1954, rolling out its overhead-valve Y-block V-8 in its stead.

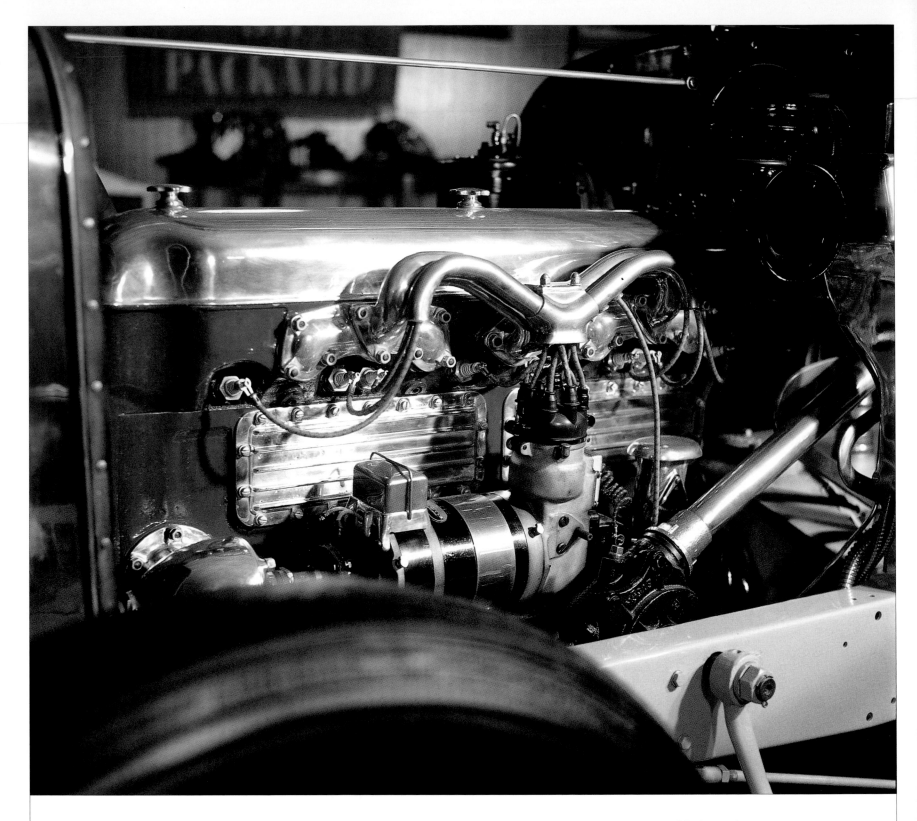

While Packard popularized the straight-eight engine during the 1920s, Duesenberg was responsible for getting the breed rolling in high style. Shown here is a 1926 Duesenberg straight eight, a 260-cubic-inch SOHC engine that produced 88 horsepower.

CHAPTER 6

Chariot of the Gods: Duesenberg Straight Eight

The brothers Duesenberg, Frederick and August, never did care much for the business end of automaking. Crossing t's and dotting i's wasn't exactly their forte; classic, state-of-the-art  engineering was—a clear testament to their German-born-and-bred heritage.

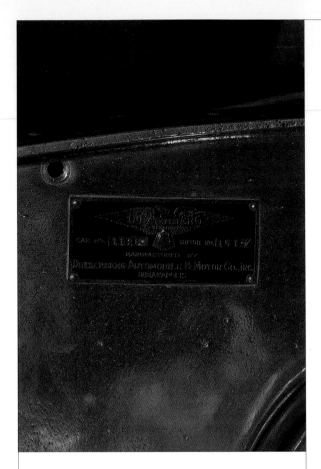

Above: The Duesenberg name was well-known in racing circles when the Indianapolis-based firm announced it would produce "The World's Champion Automobile" in 1920. A prototype straight eight model appeared that December.

Opposite, top: Model A deliveries didn't begin until late in 1921. Shown here is a rather humble (in Duesenberg terms) 1924 roadster. *Courtesy Auburn Cord Duesenberg Museum, Auburn, Indiana*

Opposite, middle: Beneath the various custom-built Duesenberg bodies was a sturdy ladder-type frame with four-wheel hydraulic brakes incorporating large 16-inch drums. Both the firewall and floor-board were cast aluminum. *Courtesy Auburn Cord Duesenberg Museum, Auburn, Indiana*

Opposite, lower: Eight-cylinder Duesenberg racers won the Indianapolis 500 in 1924, 1925, and 1927. This No. 12 Duesie, driven by Pete DePaolo, finished fifth at Indy in 1926. *Courtesy Auburn Cord Duesenberg Museum, Auburn, Indiana*

Such was the case especially for "Augie" Duesenberg. While Fred rapidly matured into one of the most prominent automotive designers of his day, his younger brother—a skilled draftsman and able designer himself—apparently preferred a hands-on approach to mechanics. Like Fred, Augie nurtured a passion for racing, and building competition machines eventually became his main claim to fame, as well as his downfall. Augie was history after mover-and-shaker Errett Lobban Cord entered the picture in 1926, essentially to save the brothers from themselves. Fred's immediate future remained in E. L. Cord's hands; Augie was simply left to find a new job building his race cars elsewhere.

Again like Fred, Augie tinkered with bicycles before both men graduated into the automotive realm about the time their first motorized creation—still a two-wheeler—appeared at the 1905 Chicago Auto Show. Fred's involvement with four-wheeled transports began in 1903, when he went to work for the Thomas B. Jeffrey Company in Kenosha, Wisconsin. He moved to Des Moines, Iowa, a few years later to, among other things, design Mason motorcars, and Augie soon joined him on staff there. Building race cars on the side quickly became job one for the brothers, and they formed their own firm in 1913, the first of various Duesenberg Motor Company iterations, to do mostly that.

A Duesenberg-powered Mason racer first appeared at the Brickyard in Indianapolis in 1912 but broke down during practice. It was fitted with the Duesenberg brothers' trademark "walking-beam" four-cylinder, a menacing racing mill that got its nickname from its nearly foot-long vertical rocker arms that actuated horizontal valves in the head from a camshaft down in the crankcase. Output was as much as 58 horsepower from as many as 243 cubic inches.

The walking-beam inline four quickly became all the rage in racing circles but never had much luck at Indy. Best finishes were 9th in 1913, 10th in 1914 (the first year for a racing machine named "Duesenberg"), and 8th in 1915. The brothers then developed a 16-valve four-cylinder, and that engine powered a Duesenberg to a second-place Indy finish in 1916. No Memorial Day races were run during 1917 and 1918 due to America's entry into World War I.

Inline eight-cylinder engines came into vogue after the war, with the Duesenbergs and racing legend Henry Miller moving to the forefront. Duesenberg's win at the French Grand Prix in 1921 shook the world. And after a Frontenac became the first straight eight to win the Indy 500 in 1921, Miller and Duesenberg eights dominated for 12 years in the American heartland before another legend, the Offenhauser four-cylinder (built by Miller), broke the string in 1937. A Miller won at Indianapolis in 1922, 1923, 1926, and from 1928 to 1936. Duesenbergs took the 500 in 1924, 1925, and 1927.

Work on the Duesenberg straight eight started in the winter of 1919. Originally displacing 297 cubic inches, the innovative engine featured a single overhead cam operating three valves per cylinder—one intake, two exhausts. Displacement was cut to 183 cubic inches after Indy officials began limiting displacement in 1920, but the downsized eight still produced upward of 115 horsepower, more than enough to make a Duesenberg racer a force to be reckoned with on the Bricks.

Yet as strong as the Duesenberg eight was, it still only powered the brothers to fame, not fortune. Winning races didn't necessarily translate into financial success for the oft-reorganized automotive venture, although that winning reputation did make it easy to attract new investors, who then supplied the cash flow to prop up a production facility that never did build enough of anything to keep its doors propped open on its own. Fred and Augie Duesenberg continued

1926 DUESENBERG STRAIGHT EIGHT

Type: water-cooled SOHC inline eight-cylinder with electric self-starting

Construction: cast-iron block and cylinder head with polished aluminum valve cover, aluminum lower crankcase/oil pan

Lubrication: fully pressurized

Main bearings: three

Bore and stroke: 2.875x5.0 inches

Displacement: 260 cubic inches

Valves: two per cylinder

Camshaft: single shaft-driven, mounted overhead of polished, spherical combustion chambers

Compression: 5:1

Induction: single-throat (1.5-inch in diameter) Schebler updraft carburetor, located on right side; fed air/fuel through block to aluminum intake manifold on left side

Ignition: Delco coil and breaker points, distributor mounted at rear of combination generator/starter

Horsepower: 88 at 3,600 rpm

engineering excellent engines for cars, boats, and a few planes. But they did so as employees for various capitalists who bought the rights to their famous family name, only to find themselves famously floundering in red ink.

By 1920, Newton Van Zandt and Luther Rankin were in charge of the newly reformed Duesenberg Automobile and Motors Corporation of Indianapolis, a firm dedicated to offering "the ultimate in motorcar design." "Built to outclass, outrun, and outlast any car on the road" this regal machine was touted as "the world's champion automobile." Many of the lessons learned by the Duesenberg brothers at the track carried over into the design and production of the first street-going automobile to bear their legendary name. Appearing first in prototype form in December 1920, the new eight-cylinder Duesenberg did not disappoint.

An American straight eight pioneer, the first Duesenberg production car also featured ground-breaking four-wheel hydraulic brakes. Its chassis rolled on a regal 134-inch wheelbase, and on top of that went various bodies supplied by various coachworks.

Displacing 260 cubic inches, the Duesenberg engine looked a lot like its racing counterparts, right down to the polished aluminum valve cover. Aluminum was used for the oil pan as well, while the cylinder block (with three main bearings) and head were typically cast iron. Polished spherical combustion chambers, pierced by inclined valves bumped by that trademark overhead cam, made up the valvetrain. Compression was 5:1, then considered quite high. Output, at 88 horsepower, was nothing to sneeze at for the time.

While the updraft carburetor was mounted on the right side of the engine below the exhaust manifold, the intake manifold itself was found on the opposite side. Air/fuel flow left the carburetor on the right, traveled through a passage in the block, and was delivered to the combustion chambers by the ram's-horn intake on the left.

As fast as it was expensive (prices began at $6,500), the well-engineered Duesenberg straight eight never found its feet, experiencing various delays going from prototype to production. Customer deliveries didn't start until late in 1921, primarily the result of the Duesenbergs'

desire to get everything right first. Sales lagged as the supposedly business-savvy managers of the company demonstrated that they too didn't know all that much about the car business. A goal of building 100 Duesenbergs each month proved far too high, as the Indianapolis plant struggled to roll out one a day. The 1922 run didn't even surpass 150, and the total score read about 650 when the Duesenberg eight was discontinued five years later.

During that span, the company had gone into receivership in 1924, and yet another reorganization followed in 1925. Along came E. L. Cord to pick up the pieces in October 1926. Cord, who only 11 months before had risen up to take control of Auburn, another Indiana automaker, was trying to build his own bold brand of automotive empire. But unlike Walter P. Chrysler, E. L. was intent on sticking solely with high rollers instead of commoners like De Soto, Dodge, and Plymouth. Purchasing Duesenberg was the latest step in Cord's plan to craft "an automobile of undisputed rank—in fact, the finest thing on four wheels."

Cord saw no place in that plan for Augie Duesenberg. Fred, however, was made vice president in charge of engineering and experimental work and charged with the task of designing E. L.'s "finest thing." The end result was, of course, the heavenly Model J, a real "Duesie" that debuted in December 1928 to redefine just how fine a fine American automobile could be. After the J's debut, the firm's original model was retroactively named "Model A."

In between the A and the J was the Model X, the little-known Duesenberg that appeared briefly in 1927. Fred and Augie had begun work on the Model X just before Cord arrived to take their surname to all new heights. Only a dozen or so Xs were built for 1927, and they marked the point in history where the brothers Duesenberg left off and E. L. Cord took off.

A new chassis with a new 135-inch wheelbase served as a foundation for the Model X, and a 100-horsepower straight eight powered it. Contrary to its cross-flow predecessor, the new OHC eight mounted both its intake and exhaust manifolds on the same side (the right) of the cylinder head, a layout first created to best incorporate the centrifugal supercharger option pioneered on a handful of Duesenberg Model As. Supercharging was planned for the Model X as well, but apparently only one such installation was made—on Fred's personal car.

A centrifugal supercharger also appeared in 1932 for the Model J's straight eight, which represented the supreme advancement of American engine design prior to World War II. Displacing 420 cubic inches, that monster relied on dual overhead cams and four valves per cylinder to produce an out-of-this-world 265 horses, at a time when Cadillac's strongest V-8 was rated at 90 horsepower. Though designed by Duesenberg, the engine was manufactured by Lycoming, another company owned by Cord.

With the blower pumping 8 pounds of boost into its slick combustion chambers, the Lycoming-supplied Model SJ eight pumped out a surreal 320 horsepower in 1932. Reportedly, an SJ was capable of reaching 100 miles per hour in a scant 17 seconds. Such performance stood light years ahead of anything seen on American roads at the time and would still elicit dropped jaws today for a machine this massive.

Only 481 Model Js were built before the A-C-D (Auburn-Cord-Duesenberg) triumvirate finally fell victim to hard economic times. Of those Model Js, 36 were supercharged SJs.

Classic simply is not a big enough word.

Opposite, top: Like its race-bred forefathers, the street-going Duesenberg straight eight relied on cutting-edge overhead-cam technology.

Opposite, lower: The straight-eight engine's carburetor was located on the right below the exhaust manifold, but its intake manifold was mounted on the opposite side. The air/fuel mixture was delivered to the intake through a passage within the cylinder block.

Left: A new straight-eight engine appeared in 1927 with both its intake and exhaust manifolds mounted on the same side. Output was 100 horsepower.

Below: Duesenberg's classic Model J appeared in December 1928 and four years later was treated to a supercharged eight that produced an unheard-of 320 horsepower. Only 481 Model J Duesenbergs were built; of these, 36 were supercharged SJ renditions. *David Kimble cutaway*

Cadillac's introduction of its V-16 in 1930 (followed immediately by a V-12) inspired Packard, Pierce-Arrow, Lincoln, and Auburn to roll out rival V-12s in 1932. Packard's 12 first measured 445 cubic inches, then was bumped up to 473 cubic inches 1935. This 1937 V-12 (missing various components, including ignition hardware) produced 175 horsepower.

CHAPTER 7

A Matter of Mathematics: Packard Twelve

Do the math: If a six beats a four, and an eight beats a six, then what beats an eight? Such was the question at Packard as World War I began.

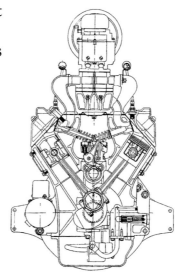

Packard defined prestige in terms of six cylinders, as did archrivals Pierce-Arrow and Peerless. But along came a relative outsider named Cadillac to change all the rules. Late in 1914, still well off the pace in America's higher-priced field, General Motors' top-shelf division traded its inadequate four cylinders for twice as many bores arranged in a V, establishing a trend that would soon sweep the industry. Peerless rolled out a new V-8 for 1916, and many others followed. Conservative Pierce-Arrow, however, stuck with its T-head six, though Chief Engineer David Fergusson did improve that engine late in 1918 by adding two more valves per cylinder.

Fergusson's counterpart at Packard, Jesse Vincent, at first considered a V-8 after word got out about Cadillac's impending milestone. But smooth, silent performance was his goal, and a V-8 vibrated a bit too much at high speeds compared to an inline six. "A six-cylinder motor is theoretically in absolutely perfect balance," he wrote early in 1915, and "this is because the vibratory forces due to the rise and fall of one piston are neutralized by equal and opposite forces due to another." Vincent also noted that a 90-degree V-8, displacing as many or more cubic inches than Packard's 414-ci inline six, would require a wider frame, which in turn would adversely affect steering geometry, making for an unwanted increase in turning radius.

On the other hand, even more cylinders of less bore diameter, arranged in a narrower V, could result in sufficient displacement that fit into a more compact space. But how many more cylinders? Ten were out of the question; they simply couldn't be balanced. Not so for a dozen. "Since a single six-cylinder motor is in perfect balance," continued Vincent, "there is no reason why we cannot combine with it another six-cylinder motor, V-type, and still have a motor that is in absolute balance." Thus came Packard's Twin Six, the industry's first viable V-12 automobile.

Right: Packard's first V-12 debuted in May 1915 in a 1916 model called, appropriately enough, the Twin Six. This 12-cylinder line was phased out in 1923 in favor of a straight-eight Packard. A new Twin Six followed in 1932 and was renamed, simply, the Packard Twelve in 1933. At left is a 1937 Packard V-12, at right is a straight eight, and behind both is a 1918 Twin Six model.

Opposite: Various improvements were made during the original Twin Six run, including a switch to detachable cylinder heads in 1917 and an output boost to 90 horsepower in 1918. Shown here is the third-series Twin Six's V-12 engine, offered from 1920 to 1923. *Photo courtesy National Automotive History Collection, Detroit Public Library*

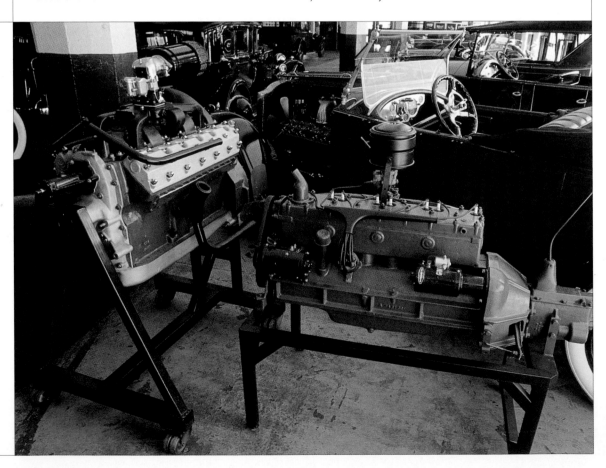

Introduced in May 1915 as a 1916 model, the Twin Six was powered by a 12-cylinder L-head that featured individually cast cylinder banks (with integral heads) opposed at a narrow 60-degree angle, resulting in 7 inches less width than a comparable 90-degree V-8. Bore was 3 inches and stroke was 5, bringing the total displacement count to 424 cubic inches. Water-cooled and pressure-lubricated, this mighty engine was fed by a single updraft carburetor and featured a pair of distributors—one for each bank of six cylinders. A short, lightweight crankshaft was held in place by three main bearings.

Output was a resounding 88 horsepower, compared to the 65 delivered by the retiring straight six, which outweighed its successor by 400 pounds. More important was the V-12's newfound torque, which, according to Vincent, was "50 percent better than it would have been with a V-8 and 100 percent better than the Packard Six."

A three-speed transmission typically went behind this V-12, but why? Launching in third was no problem for the Twin Six, as witnesses quickly discovered. "Perhaps the most remarkable feature of the running is that there is no sense of effort whatever in opening up from 3 (miles per hour) on high gear," reported *The Automobile*. "In a series of trials run against the watch, it was found that it was easy to accelerate from 3 miles an hour to 30 miles in 12 seconds on a level cement road and on second speed in a much shorter time. It is not likely that the low gears would be used for more than a decimal percentage of the running."

As soft-spoken as it was strong, the Twin Six also impressed bystanders with the way all that stump-pulling power simply purred. "Six impulses per crankshaft revolution blend together so closely as to make it absolutely impossible to distinguish any pause between impulses, even at very low engine speeds," bragged Vincent. "The only thing I can liken it to is the action of steam."

"No vibration was perceptible up to a road speed of well over 60 miles per hour," added Great Britain's *The Automobile*, "and the motor is hardly audible even at full revolutions."

Packard built more than 35,000 Twin Six models between 1916 and 1923, with improvements including detachable cylinder heads in 1917 and an increase to 90 horsepower for 1918. Unfortunately, demand began to wane during the 1920s, especially so after Packard introduced its downsized Single Six for 1921. Duesenberg's fabulous overhead-cam straight eight also debuted about that time, inspiring major interest in the new layout. Packard countered next with its own inline eight, an L-head that appeared in June 1923 (as a 1924 model) to replace the fading Twin Six.

Countless other straight eights quickly emerged as American automakers basically forgot all about the V-12 concept. As it was, the only substantial rival to the Twin Six was National's "Highway Twelve," which also debuted in May 1915. It was canceled in 1919. Cincinnati-based Enger too offered a V-12, in 1916 and 1917. Meanwhile, over in Kokomo, Indiana, Haynes was rolling out its own V-12, introduced as well in 1916, but only about 650 were built before the model line ceased in 1922, three years before the factory itself was shuttered.

Really big cylinder counts didn't come back into vogue until Cadillac introduced its really big V-16 in 1930, followed the next year by a new V-12. Though Marmon countered with its own 16, remaining luxury rivals opted for the less lavish 12, including Pierce-Arrow, Lincoln, and Auburn in 1932 and Franklin in 1933. Packard then got its face back in the race, introducing a second Twin Six in January 1932.

That second time, Jesse Vincent had hired an outside contractor, Cornelius Van Ranst, to oversee his company's new V-12. Van Ranst's resume was rich in racing experience, including

1937 PACKARD V-12

Type: water-cooled 67-degree V-12 L-head

Construction: cast-iron monobloc with detachable aluminum heads

Lubrication: fully pressurized

Main bearings: four

Bore and stroke: 3.4375x4.250 inches

Displacement: 473 cubic inches

Valves: two per cylinder, 1.5 inches in diameter; intakes made of nickel steel, exhausts of silicon chrome

Camshaft: single with hydraulic valve silencers

Compression: 6:1 standard, 6.4:1 and 7:1 optional

Induction: dual-throat Bendix-Stromberg downdraft carburetor with automatic choke control

Ignition: Autolite distributor

Horsepower: 175 at 3,200 rpm (180 with optional high-compression head)

Torque: 366 at 1,400 rpm

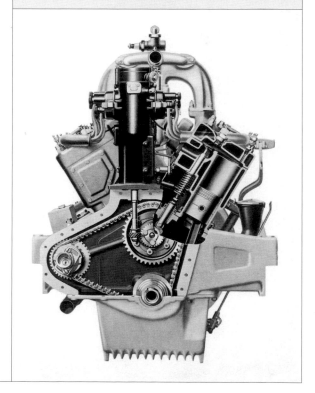

Packard's third-series Twin Six models rode on a 136-inch wheelbase. Shown here is a 1920–1923 five-passenger phaeton. *Photo courtesy National Automotive History Collection, Detroit Public Library*

Notice the second-edition Twin Six engine's unique valve layout (with roller-tipped rocker arms and hydraulic tappet silencers) and integral cylinder block construction. A dual-throat Stromberg downdraft carburetor supplied the air/fuel mixture.

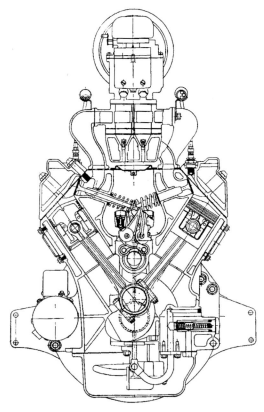

time with Duesenberg and Louis Chevrolet. He also built a front-wheel-drive racer for GM founder William Durant's son Russell in 1927, and followed that up with a tour at Cord, where he helped create the fabulous front-driven L-29. After Cord's classic L-29 debuted in 1929, Packard people became interested in producing a competing front-driver, and Van Ranst was brought in to do just that. That model never made it into production. But its engine did.

As different from Packard's original V-12 as night is to day, the second Twin Six engine featured four main bearings, and its cylinder banks and crankcase were cast integrally in one sturdy iron block, something only the Marmon V-16 claimed at that time in Detroit's most luxurious ranks. Additional innovations included hydraulic tappet silencers (borrowed from Cadillac's V-16) and a dual-throat Bendix-Stromberg downdraft carburetor, itself pioneered by Chrysler in 1928 and used again atop Marmon's 16. While Marmon relied on a DDR-3 model, Van Ranst chose a new, modified Stromberg, the EE-3, with automatic choke control.

With a bore of 3.4375 inches and a stroke of 4 inches, this 67-degree L-head V-12 displaced 445 cubic inches and produced 160 healthy horses. Valves measured 1.5 inches in diameter, with the intakes made of nickel steel, the exhausts silicon chrome. While Van Ranst's prototype engine design featured dual distributors, a single Autolite unit became the standard in production. Detachable cast-iron heads topped things off, bringing compression to 6.0:1. New aluminum heads appeared in 1934 with either the stock 6.0:1 compression or a higher 6.8:1 squeeze.

A new name also appeared in 1933, as Packard people apparently didn't want customers to think they were simply getting a rehash of what they'd last seen 10 years before. Simply called the Packard Twelve, 1933's engine was the same as 1932's, save for revised cooling. But big changes did come in 1935, as engineers strove to make the Twelve a better match for the V-16 Caddie. Stroke was stretched to 4.25 inches, resulting in a boost up to 473 cubic inches. Output in turn rose to 175 horsepower, 180 with high-compression heads. Two optional ratios were offered from 1935 to 1936: 6.25:1 and 7.0:1. Beginning in 1937, the choices were 6.4:1 and 7.0:1.

Standard with the Packard Twelve was the company's "Certificate of Approval," which, among other things, stated that each car had been driven around Packard Proving Grounds for 250 miles. Before that, each engine, upon assembly, was run for an hour by electric motor, followed by six more hours on its own. Yet another 1.25 hours then followed on the dynamometer.

A completely different, if not downright oddball, test also occurred at the Packard Proving Grounds in July 1932, when legendary golfer and longtime Packard owner Gene Sarazen pitted one of his classic tee shots against an equally classic Twin Six speedster driven by Jesse Vincent. It was left to the *Detroit News* to recount the epic showdown.

"Impelled by the force of Sarazen's unerring swing, the ball shot out in front of the car. Then its slowly spending force became apparent against the relentlessly speeding car, which Vincent's foot was keeping unvarying at 120 miles an hour. There was a space of many yards when the car and ball were racing on even terms. Gradually, the car pulled away, its wraithlike length moving out in front of the little white sphere." Reportedly, Sarazen's ball traveled 230 yards in 4.5 seconds, while the Packard needed only 4.1 clicks to cover the same distance.

Packard built 5,804 more V-12s between 1932 and 1939, all of them tremendous automobiles. Just ask the golfer who owned one.

All V-12 Packards were fabulous automobiles, but did it get any better than this 1934 Twelve roadster? A rumble seat in back expanded available seating from two to four.

Aluminum heads were new atop Packard's 160-horsepower, 445-cubic-inch V-12 in 1934.

Packard gained the upper hand during the 1920s in Detroit's luxury ranks with its powerful straight-eight models. Cadillac then doubled up on its rival in 1930 with its classic V-16 cars. Cadillac's narrow-angle (45-degree) V-16 displaced 452 cubic inches.

CHAPTER 8

Sweet Sixteen: Cadillac V-16

"It was the best of times; it was the worst of times." Charles Dickens'
paradoxical prose easily could've passed for
the opening line to the tale of one American
city's trials and tribulations during the
Great Depression.

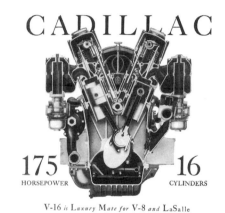

V-16 *is Luxury Mate for* V-8 *and* LaSalle

1930 CADILLAC V-16

Type: water-cooled OHV 45-degree V-16

Construction: cast-iron individual cylinder banks and heads, two-piece aluminum crankcase

Lubrication: fully pressurized

Main bearings: five

Bore and stroke: 3.0x4.0 inches

Displacement: 452 cubic inches

Valves: two per cylinder

Camshaft: single with hydraulic valve silencers

Compression: 5.5:1

Induction: two updraft carburetors, mounted outboard of cylinder banks

Ignition: Delco-Remy dual-breaker distributor

Horsepower: 165 at 3,400 rpm

"Awesome" simply was not a big enough word in the V-16 Cadillac's case. Various models were offered, including this 1931 dual-cowl phaeton, which, in its day, redefined America's perception of power and prestige. *David Kimble cutaway*

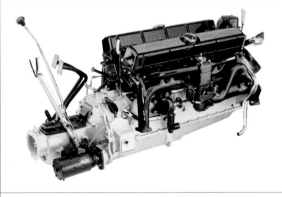

Each of the Cadillac V-16's cylinder banks was treated as a separate straight eight as far as fuel delivery was concerned. Two updraft carburetors were used. *Steve and Pattie Constable photo, courtesy of General Motors*

Detroit, the long-established hub of this country's automaking universe, was host to delight and despair in the 1930s, each in historic portions, with this duality primarily evident at the industry's upper crust. At a time when so many companies could barely afford to stay in business, some were still busy crafting the most luxurious, most memorable motorcars ever, and it cost them dearly. Fine-car firms, including Cadillac, Chrysler, and Lincoln, lost money by the wheelbarrow-load in the years after the 1929 stock market crash.

But, backed up by Big-Three bucks, that familiar trio never was in danger of failing. The remaining independents, however, were not so fortunate. Packard, America's premier luxury nameplate heading into the 1930s, managed to survive the Depression but was never the same again. Other high-rollers simply succumbed then and there. Duesenberg, Pierce-Arrow, Marmon, Peerless, Franklin, and Stutz were all dead and buried before the decade was out.

How surreal it must have been—American automotive artistry reaching its zenith, high above such harsh realities in a rose-colored stratosphere, during an epoch known better for soup lines, dust bowls, and shattered dreams. From that dark decade came some of automotive history's best and brightest: magnificent motoring marvels like the supercharged Duesenberg J and the various V-12 showboats from Packard, Pierce-Arrow, and Lincoln. And lest we forget the supreme dream machine that set the pace for all other 1930s classics to follow: the wretchedly excessive Cadillac V-16.

Introduced at the New York Automobile Show on January 4, 1930, this colossus was created to prove once and for all that both Cadillac and the V-type engines it concentrated on were tops in the U.S. luxury market. During the 1920s, the straight eight had settled in as the popular choice for the rich and famous, with Packard leading the way, though not for long. Unseating Packard became Lawrence Fisher's main goal after rising to the general manager's throne at Cadillac in April 1925, and the V-16 represented an exclamation point to his goal.

Sixteen-cylinder mills had been seen on racetracks before, but no one had dared to try to put one into regular production. Cadillac Chief Engineer Ernest Seaholm assigned the task to experienced engine man Owen Nacker, who had joined the firm in 1926. Though a V-12 was developed under Nacker's direction to help put Packard in its place, Fisher and his officers determined that even those extra four cylinders were not enough to do the job. Beating the opposition wasn't sufficient; beating it to a pulp was more like it. Thus emerged the cylinder count to end all cylinder counts.

"The justification for the existence of the V-16 passenger car engine was—like many other factors in life, industry, and war—purely psychological," wrote noted automotive historian Griffith Borgeson in *Automobile Quarterly* in 1984. "The sixteen is, uncontestably and overwhelmingly, The Most."

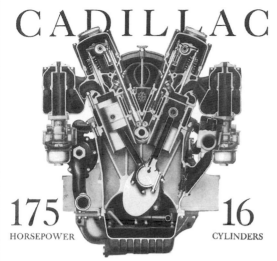

CADILLAC

175 HORSEPOWER 16 CYLINDERS

V-16 *is Luxury Mate for* V-8 *and* LaSalle

Right: Cutting-edge aspects included overhead valves with hydraulic silencers. Initial output in 1930 was 165 horsepower, but that increased to 175 in 1934 and 185 in 1936.

Below: Various sources supplied bodies for Cadillac's long list of V-16 models, including this 1930 phaeton coachwork.

Above: Cadillac's V-16 was a work of art from both an engineering and aesthetic point of view. Complemented by tasteful chrome, polished aluminum, and gleaming black enamel, it was America's first fashion-conscious engine.

Opposite, lower: Cadillac replaced its modern OHV V-16 in 1938 with an old-fashioned L-head V-16, which remained in production until 1940. Notice the twin side-by-side downdraft carburetors. *Steve and Pattie Constable photo, courtesy of General Motors*

Opposite, top: Cadillac's nearly flat L-head V-16 was laid out on a 135-degree angle. Displacement was 431 cubic inches; output was 185 horsepower.

The V-16 also rated as a milestone for reasons beyond its record number of cylinders. "Among automotive powerplants, it stands uniquely alone—not only the first of its kind to be produced but entirely unchallenged from the standpoint of its general excellence," claimed a classic Cadillac advertisement from 1930. By then, General Motors had already become known as the industry's unquestioned leader in design and engineering, and Cadillac's new overhead-valve V-16 engine stood as an epitome in both areas.

Sixteen cylinders weren't chosen solely to double the ante on Packard; they were put into play because of their inherent smoothness. Thanks to all those extra firings, a V-16 naturally purrs like a kitten, and Cadillac had many owners wondering if their little fur-ball was running in its sleep. Adding to the illusion was the engine's ultraquiet operation, assured by the pioneering use of hydraulic valve silencers, innovations that used oil pressure to automatically reset valve lash at zero. Previous OHV designs had required constant manual adjustments to keep their valves from clacking due to unwanted expanding clearances. Cadillac's design did away with both the noise and the maintenance hassle and represented the precursor to the modern hydraulic lifter that soon emerged to solve this problem in all OHV engines.

Cadillac's V-16 also demonstrated general excellence in its outward appearance. That aforementioned ad wasn't titled "Works of the Modern Masters" for nothing. Along with being an engineering masterpiece, the history-making motor also looked as pretty as a painting with its combination of dazzling chrome, polished aluminum, and jet-black enamel. All wiring and plumbing was perfectly hidden to heighten the focus on the star of the underhood show. Packard's (and Duesenberg's) gloriously green eights were no slouches when it came to catching the eye, but Cadillac's V-16 was the first American engine to actually feel a substantial stylist's touch.

Beneath all that beauty was a narrow-angle (45-degree) V-16 that featured separate heads, cylinder blocks, and crankcase. The latter structure, made in two parts, was aluminum, as were the flashy valve covers, while the remaining pieces were cast from nickel-iron. A counterweighted crankshaft was held in place by five main bearings and featured a small vibration damper up front, all the better to make this sweet 16 run even smoother. With a bore of 3 inches and a stroke of 4, displacement came to 452 cubic inches. Compression was 5.5:1, and maximum output was 165 horsepower at 3,400 rpm.

Each cylinder bank was treated as an individual straight eight for fuel delivery. Two separate vacuum tanks and two updraft carburetors were used, with the latter equipment mounted outboard of each head, along with the two exhaust manifolds. Keeping the center of the V clear of obstructions was preferred in those days from a servicing standpoint and was more aesthetically pleasing. Sending sparks to those 16 plugs was the job of a Delco-Remy dual-breaker distributor.

Introduced in July 1930, Cadillac's new V-12 was more or less a V-16 with four cylinders and one main bearing lopped off. The two shared many parts, and the V-12 was predictably less mighty: 370 cubic inches and 135 horsepower. Going into smaller, less expensive Cadillacs, the V-12 unfortunately stole some of the V-16's thunder. The company sold 1,984 1931 V-12s during the model's first six months on the market, and there's no telling how many of those customers (as well as those who followed) might have considered the supreme Cadillac had the 12 not come along. As it was, V-16 production that first year was 2,887, certainly a grand number considering the sorry economic state at the time and the royal ransom required to take one home. A V-16 roadster started at $5,325, and the pricing pecking order peaked at $9,700 for the wholly ostentatious Town Brougham.

V-16 demand quickly nosedived from there, with the total number sold from 1930 to 1937 amounting to nearly 3,900. Improvements along the way included output increases to 175 horsepower in 1934 and 185 in 1936. Then, in 1938, Cadillac traded its thoroughly modern OHV V-16 for an L-head 16 laid out at a much flatter 135-degree angle. Created with economics in mind, that second-generation V-16 featured less than half the parts contained in its predecessor and displaced 431 cubic inches. Output was also 185 horsepower. Twin downdraft carburetors were new, but the "flathead" 16 paled in comparison to its OHV forerunner in terms of sheer eye-appeal. Only 508 models were built before 1940, when the V-16 legacy ended.

Reportedly, Cadillac lost money on every V-16 model it built. By the end of 1930, GM reports showed a $54 million investment in the V-12/V-16 project, and many more millions awaited further investing. The total retail value of the OHV V-16 cars sold from 1930 to 1937 was about $20 million, and their V-12 running mates brought in about twice that during the same time span.

But the V-16 wasn't about making money; it was given another job entirely: to carry Cadillac to the top from a purely prestigious perspective. That it did, just as Larry Fisher planned.

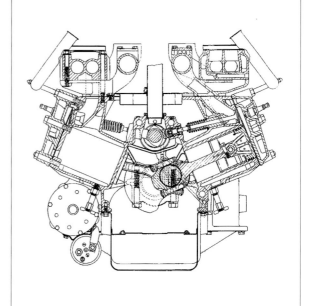

The Offenhauser four-cylinder's competition career spanned a half-century, during which time it was built in countless forms. Shown here is the injected 270 derivative. In the background is Parnelli Jones' Offy roadster, which won the Indianapolis 500 in 1963 with an average speed of 143.137 miles per hour.

CHAPTER 9

Hittin' the Bricks: Offenhauser Racing Four-Cylinder

One of America's greatest engines never made it to American streets.

Known both affectionately and reverently as the

"Offy," this overhead-cam four-cylinder still

stands as the most dominating, longest-running

racing mill to ever hit the bricks at Indianapolis.

OFFENHAUSER 270

Type: water-cooled DOHC inline four-cylinder

Construction: aluminum barrel-type crankcase, one-piece cast-iron cylinder block/head, pent-roof combustion chambers with centrally located spark plugs

Lubrication: high-pressure dry sump

Main bearings: five, located in removable webs

Bore and stroke: 4.3125x4.625 inches

Displacement: 270 cubic inches

Valves: four per cylinder

Camshaft: dual overhead, driven by multiple gears in gear tower

Compression: varied, 15:1 common

Induction: Hilborn fuel injection

Ignition: Joe Hunt magneto

Horsepower: varied, 325 listed initially

Though displacement varied and various induction systems were used over the years, the Offy's basic layout prevailed: dual overhead cams activated four valves in each cylinder. *David Kimble cutaway*

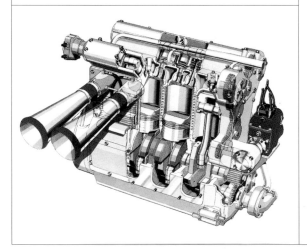

Its on-track successes spanned a half-century, a truly remarkable achievement that without a doubt will never be matched as long as competition machines continue making left turn after left turn.

An Offy first won the Indy 500 in 1934, kicking off an almost-unchallenged dynasty that wasn't seriously dented until Henry Ford II invested many millions in a balls-out four-cam V-8 and dropped one of these into Jim Clark's Lotus, which won on the Bricks in 1965. But even Ford's big-buck challenge couldn't completely derail the venerable Offy four, which made a couple of comebacks at the Brickyard before finally retiring from the Indy scene 15 years later.

The full name was Offenhauser, after Fred Offenhauser, the highly talented machinist most responsible for its creation. A date of birth for the Offenhauser racing engine is not easy to specify, because this diehard four-cylinder wasn't necessarily conceived overnight; it evolved during a protracted development stage, and it continued evolving throughout its long career.

Even its name took its sweet time coming into vogue. Offenhauser worked for Harry Miller when he first put the Offy wheels in motion during the late 1920s, and all early engines were labeled "Millers." That tag stuck even after Miller's legendary race shop in Los Angeles went bankrupt in 1933 and Offenhauser himself took over production. The Offenhauser Engineering Company opened for business in 1934, but it wasn't until the following year that Fred's surname first appeared at Indy, officially attached to the mean little four-cylinder that was kicking ass and taking names practically everywhere it went.

When Indianapolis legend Louie Meyer entered his Ring-Free Special in the 1936 Memorial Day race, he simply couldn't call a spade a spade. Official paperwork identified the twin-cam four-cylinder that powered him to an unprecedented third Indy 500 victory that year as a Miller. As Meyer later told veteran racing historian and *Automobile Quarterly* contributor Spencer Riggs, "There never was an Offenhauser engine. No matter what name you call it, it's still Harry Miller's design."

Meyer meant no disrespect. He was just pointing out that Fred Offenhauser wasn't solely responsible for the race engine that eventually bore his name and kept it through the years, regardless of who actually was responsible for further development. On that list was Meyer himself, who, along with Dale Drake, bought out Offenhauser after he retired in 1946. Though technically a Meyer-Drake engine, the dominating four-cylinder was still commonly called an Offenhauser at the track, and that traditional tag remained long after Meyer left the firm and the renamed Drake Engineering Company took over in 1965. Meyer, Drake, and various others (A. J. Watson and Art Sparks, to name a couple) continued developing the engine, sometimes quite radically, but the Offenhauser title still stuck in race fans' minds.

Also important to the Offy's conception was Miller employee Leo Goossen, who ended up keeping his finger on that engine's pulse for nearly 50 years. Goossen also preferred to spread the credit around. As he told *True* magazine contributor Griffith Borgeson in 1956, "Fred, Miller, and I were only a part of a design team. Ever since Harry and Fred made carburetors back in the Teens, the (Miller Manufacturing) shop was (West) Coast headquarters for all the boys in the racing fraternity, and every one of 'em—(Ralph) De Palma, (Jimmy) Murphy, (Frank) Lockhart, and all the rest—gave us ideas. A lot of the time the biggest job Fred or Harry or I had was to sift the ideas that other people gave us and choose the good ones."

But from there it apparently was Offenhauser who did the bulk of the sifting.

"Fred had been working for Miller long before the Old Man ever considered building an engine," added Borgeson in his January 1956 *True* article, titled "America's Four-Barreled Bomb."

"And through the years, he became one of the few men who dared to look at one of Miller's sketches and say, 'Harry, you just can't build it that way. It won't work.' Although Miller ruled—sometimes erratically—in the drafting room, Fred, for decades, was undisputed bull-of-the-woods in the shop."

Originally hired by Miller in late 1913, Fred Offenhauser was primarily responsible for Miller Manufacturing's first engine, an overhead-cam six-cylinder ordered by San Francisco aviator Silas Christofferson in 1914. After building an impressive racing mill for famed racer Bob Burman (who lost his life in the resulting machine) in 1915, the Miller team began concentrating its efforts on the legendary straight eight engines that began dominating the Indy 500 in 1922. Miller eights repeated as Indy champs in 1923, 1926, and from 1928 to 1933.

By 1956, Offy-powered racers had claimed 14 of the previous 17 Indy 500s, and the remaining 1950s 500-milers then also went to Offenhauser. Back in 1954, all 33 Indianapolis starters relied on Offy engines, a first-time feat repeated in 1955, 1959, and 1960. From 1946 to 1963, nearly all AAA/USAC Championship Division races were won by the four-cylinder powerplant originally built by the Harry A. Miller Manufacturing Company.

While additional four-cylinder experimentation was done during the early 1920s, serious Offy racing development dates back to 1926, when Dick Loynes contracted Miller to build a four-banger for his racing boat. The resulting 151-cubic-inch Miller Marine four became an instant winner on water and attracted promoter Bill White, who was looking for something capable of running with the modified four-barrel Fords then dominating dirt tracks. White put a Miller Marine engine in a car and clocked 144.894 at southern California's Muroc Dry Lake. He then took a modified 183-ci marine motor (known as the Miller-Schofield after George Schofield bought into the Miller firm in February 1929) to Indianapolis in 1930, where Shorty Cantlon drove it to a surprising second-place finish.

The Offenhauser legacy was kicked off by this Miller Marine four-cylinder, developed in the late 1920s. It displaced 151 cubic inches and made as much as 188 horsepower. Notice the centrifugal supercharger. *Photo courtesy Spencer Riggs*

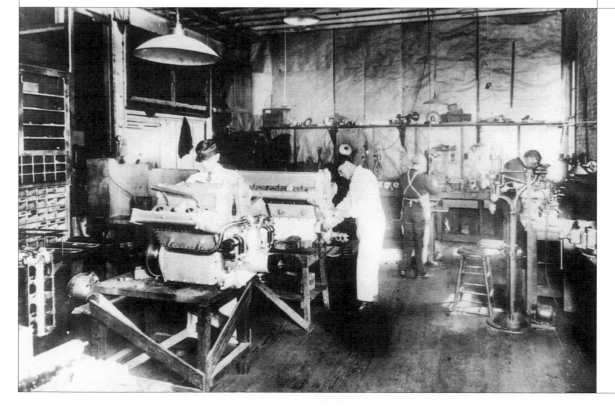

Harry A. Miller Manufacturing, located in Los Angeles, was home to both the Miller Marine four-cylinder and various Indy-winning straight eights during the 1920s. Miller eights won the Indianapolis 500 in 1922, 1923, 1926, and from 1928 to 1933. *Photo courtesy Spencer Riggs*

Fuel-injected Offys began showing up at Indy in 1948. In 1952, Bill Vukovich dominated the 500 in his Howard Keck Fuel-Injection Special, leading 140 laps before a steering failure ruined his day. Troy Ruttman's injected Offy won that year's race. *Photo courtesy Spencer Riggs*

A 270 Offy is readied for battle at Indianapolis in 1953. *Photo courtesy Spencer Riggs*

By year's end, Miller, Offenhauser, and Goossen had morphed the marine engine into a 200-cubic-inch four that further cemented Offy development. Like its floating forerunner, the 200 featured an aluminum barrel-type crankcase, an integral cylinder block/head cast in iron, two overhead cams, and centrally located spark plugs. Setting the 200 apart were its four-valve pent-roof combustion chambers (as opposed to the two-valve hemispherical chambers used previously), a narrower valve inclination angle, a modified short-throw chrome molybdenum steel crankshaft held in place by five main bearings, wider poured babbit bearings, and a relocated magneto (from the right side to the left).

Gear-driven Winfield cams were the norm from the start, as were twin Miller carburetors. Riley or Winfield carbs soon replaced the Miller pots, and those mixers sent air/fuel to intake valves measuring 1.5 inches. Exhausts were 1.375 inches in diameter. Bore and stroke measurements were 3.875 and 4.250 inches, respectively, and a dry-sump system handled lubrication.

Expanding that bore to 4.0625 inches resulted in the 220 Offy in 1932, and a stroke stretch the following year produced the 255, which pumped out 250 horsepower. Increasing both bore and stroke in 1937 resulted in the 270, able to make 300 horses. Countless other output levels and cubic-inch counts appeared over the years, including a tiny 97-incher that ruled midget racing from 1934 well into the 1970s. All told, Offy displacements over the years went from as low as 85 cubic inches to as high as 318. Compression too varied widely, from a 12:1 squeeze for the original 200 all the way up to a crushing 17:1 in the 1960s. Compression levels understandably started dropping back down (to 8:1) once turbocharging and supercharging entered into the equation. Variations also included some eight-valve Offys. Valve inclination varied all over the place, and late Offenhauser engines were laid down on their sides for a lower body profile.

After 1948, carburetors began fading away in favor of Hilborn injectors, a move that reportedly upped output by 30 horsepower. As it was, methanol-fed 255 Offys were making as many as 370 horses by the mid-1950s. A. J. Watson banked on a shorter stroke for his cleverly modified 252-cubic-inch Offy engines, which were blasting out 450 horsepower by the early 1960s. Watson's Offenhauser hybrids won every Indy 500 from 1959 to 1964.

A. J. Foyt's win in 1964 signaled the end for the traditional front-engine roadster at the Brickyard and represented the last Memorial Day victory for a normally aspirated Offy. As early as 1950, Meyer-Drake had tried supercharging a 176.8-cubic-inch twin-cam four, and Herb Porter later managed to induce 575 horsepower from a 170-ci variant of that blown engine. Few witnesses paid much notice to such gains then, but it had become clear that the Offenhauser's future hinged on a major power boost after Ford engines won three straight Indy 500s from 1965 to 1967.

By that time, a Roots-blown 170-ci Offenhauser had shown 545 horsepower on a Champion Spark Plug dyno. To match such experiments, Dale Drake and Leo Goossen put their heads together to develop an all-new twin-cam four able to handle as many as 9,000 rpm. With a rev-conscious short stroke (3.125 inches) coupled with a 4.125-inch bore, this 168-cubic-inch powerplant was the first oversquare Offy, and it also featured the breed's first aluminum block, which was 2.375 inches shorter than its predecessor.

Though this engine did appear with forced induction, a less-complicated turbocharger was used in place of the Roots-type compressor. Working with injector man Stu Hilborn and the AiResearch people, Herb Porter put together a turbo Offy good for 600 horsepower. Key to that package was an AiResearch TE06 turbocharger that delivered 15 to 20 pounds of boost.

Top: A Joe Hunt magneto was a popular ignition source for the 270 Offy.

Above: Offenhauser construction featured a cast-iron cylinder block bolted up to an aluminum barrel-type crankcase. Lubrication was supplied by a typical high-pressure, dry-sump system.

Meyer-Drake took over Offenhauser production after Fred Offenhauser retired in 1946. The company name then became simply Drake Engineering in 1965. Notice the turbocharger appearing in this 1969 Drake ad; the last normally aspirated Offy to win at Indy was A. J. Foyt's in 1964. *Photo courtesy Spencer Riggs*

Initial tests resulted in melted valves, but the chief engineer who had more experience with the Offenhauser four than any other man, quickly solved that problem. Having stuck with his pride and joy from Miller to Offenhauser Engineering to Meyer-Drake to Drake Engineering, Leo Goossen was there through every twist and turn, including the final leg of the journey, as the engine rushed into the turbo age.

Among Goossen's turbo tweaks were a compression cut (from 8:1 to 7:1) and a boost limit of 17 psi. The final product produced 625 horsepower, roughly 125 horses more than the dominating Fords were capable of, and that advantage instantly translated into an Indy 500 win in 1968 for Bobby Unser's Eagle-Offy. Unser's average speed, 152.882 miles per hour, was a record at Indianapolis.

Ford-powered machines retaliated with another three straight wins, beginning in 1969, though the old champ was not far behind. In 1971, Peter Revson's McLaren-Offy finished second after starting in the pole position with a qualifying record speed of 178.696 miles per hour. By then, AiResearch had developed a new turbocharger with 20 percent more pumping power, meaning it spun less fiercely to create maximum boost—23 pounds in this case. When bolted to a new 159-ci Offy, the end result was 730 horsepower at 8,500 rpm. With that engine, Mark Donahue's McLaren-Offy won the 1972 500-miler, averaging 162.962 miles per hour, a record that would stand until 1984.

Nine of the top 10 Indy finishers in 1973 were Offenhausers, with Gordon Johncock's Offy taking the rain-shortened race. Johnny Rutherford's McLaren-Offy established a new qualifying standard that year of 198.413 miles per hour, and his best lap of 199.071 represented the fastest an Offenhauser-powered racing machine would ever run. Three more Indianapolis wins followed for the turbocharged twin-cam four in 1974, 1975, and 1976, before the curtain finally began to drop.

Earlier, Art Sparks had teamed up with Goossen and Dale Drake to produce a new Offy called the "DGS" (Drake-Goossen-Sparks) engine. But Drake passed away in 1972, and the DGS

Turbocharged Fords won the Indianapolis 500 from 1969 to 1971, then along came Roger Penske's McLaren/Offy. Driven by Mark Donahue, this machine won the 1972 500 with an average speed of 162.962 miles per hour, a record that stood until 1984. *Photo courtesy Spencer Riggs*

motor was still on the drawing board when Leo Goossen followed him two years later. "Many old-timers claim the Offy died with him," wrote Spencer Riggs, concerning Goossen's death in *Automobile Quarterly* in 1993. An Offenhauser would never again win the Indy 500, and the breed last toured the Brickyard in 1980.

Fifty years between its first and last showings at Indianapolis. Countless wins and speed records in all kinds of American oval racing, on both paved tracks and dirt. Talk about a great engine.

Gary Bettenhausen's DGS Offy stormed from 32nd to 3rd at Indianapolis in 1980, a legendary run that served as a suitable sendoff for the Offenhauser four-cylinder, which would never hit the bricks again. *Photo courtesy Spencer Riggs*

Known for campaigning Chrysler's hemi-head V-8 early on, Briggs Cunningham turned to Offenhauser power for his C-6R racer in 1955. Installing the 183-cubic-inch Offy four beneath the C-6R's low hood required that the engine be slanted 12 degrees to the left.

Both Cadillac and Oldsmobile introduced modern overhead-valve V-8s for 1949, with the former's displacing 331 cubic inches. Oldsmobile's high-winding Rocket V-8 displaced 303 cubic inches. Output was 135 horsepower.

CHAPTER 10

Blast Off: Oldsmobile Rocket V-8

Start talking muscle cars and the conversation usually begins with Pontiac's

1964 GTO, considered in most schools of

thought today to be the founding member of

this high-powered fraternity. Granted, the so-

called "Goat" was the first of a new, modern

breed of factory hot rod, and for that it

certainly does deserve milestone status. But

the basic idea behind this ground-breaking

ground-pounder wasn't necessarily new.

Various Oldsmobiles have paced the Indianapolis 500 over the years, with a Rocket 88 convertible becoming the first in 1949. Legendary Indy driver Wilbur Shaw handled pace car piloting chores that year.

Pontiac's quick thinkers created the GTO by stuffing a lot of engine into not a lot of car and letting physical laws take over from there. Sound familiar? Veteran Buick people might've thought so. Back in 1936, the gentlemen from Flint had introduced their Century, which used the big, heavy Roadmaster's powerful overhead-valve straight eight in a platform based on the less-hefty Special's shorter wheelbase. This simple mixing and matching immediately made the Buick Century one of Detroit's toughest cars to beat on the street.

A second mover and shaker that might qualify as a forefather to the GTO came in 1949, again from General Motors. "Make a date with a Rocket 88," was Oldsmobile's invitation to take this little number out on the town, and that name couldn't have been any more appropriate.

"The Rocket 88 is as hot as a hornet's kiss," claimed *Mechanix Illustrated* road tester Tom McCahill in 1950. McCahill also labeled the 88 Olds "the best all-around highway-performing production car made in America today." At 12 seconds, its 0–60 clocking was outstanding for the time, certainly so for a four-door sedan, which McCahill tested. But the number that probably impressed more *Mechanix Illustrated* readers was the Rocket 88's top end: 96.9 miles per hour. Triple digits on the speedometer still represented rarified air (any guesses as to where Buick got the "Century" name?) then, and 96.9 was close enough to that magic barrier to make really big news.

How'd the good Olds guys do it? Creating that muscular machine was again a matter of combining more with less. When the 1949 model year began, Oldsmobile showed off two model lines: the lighter, less expensive 76 and the big, plush 98. The former rolled on 119.5-inch wheelbase, the latter 125 inches. Standard for the 76 was Oldsmobile's 105-horsepower "Big Six" L-head. But beneath the "Futuramic" 98's hood, in place of the 257-ci L-head straight eight last seen in 1948, was the truly new, truly modern Rocket V-8, a 303-cubic-incher rated at a sensational (for the day) 135 horsepower. That stunner was introduced in November 1948. In February 1949, word got out that Olds engineers had planted their V-8 into the comparatively lithe 76 platform—bam, enter the Rocket 88.

Oldsmobile had built V-8s before (1916–1923), so the Rocket engine's introduction didn't make company history as far as basic layout was concerned. But there was no comparison between what came before and what wowed Olds customers in 1949. Like Cadillac's new V-8 that year, the Rocket was an overhead-valve motor that could wind up like nothing else, thanks to its cutting-edge short stroke. Higher rev limits generally mean high power potential, and shorter strokes translate into more rpm due to the plain fact that the pistons and connecting rods involved don't have to move around as much while reciprocating, compared to their long-stroke counterparts.

On the other hand, longer strokes mean more torque—just the ticket to get heavy cars up hills, a task that wasn't all that easy for many machines prior to 1920. Really long strokes prevailed in those days for that reason and others, not the least of which involved basic design parameters. Displacement is, of course, a function of bore and stroke: increasing both of these factors at the same time or either one while keeping the other constant always has and always will translate into more cubic inches. But inline engine designs can only accept so much bore diameter before growing too long for their engine compartments. Consequently, it became the crankshaft's responsibility to maximize displacement in an inline six or eight.

Fitting many more cubic inches into a much smaller space represented the prime attraction of the V-8 design in its earliest days—that, and the fact that this compact engine

Some old-timers say that the Rocket 88 was Detroit's first muscle car. Its exceptional power-to-weight ratio certainly stood head and shoulders above anything else available in America in 1949.

Olds Rockets were big winners on NASCAR tracks in 1949 and 1950.

1949 OLDS ROCKET 88

Type: water-cooled OHV 90-degree V-8

Construction: cast-iron block and heads

Main bearings: five

Bore and stroke: 3.75x3.4375 inches

Displacement: 303 cubic inches

Valves: two per cylinder, activated by rocker arms on central pivot shaft

Lifters: hydraulic

Compression: 7.25:1

Induction: single Carter two-barrel carburetor on dual-plane intake manifold

Exhaust: single muffler and tailpipe

Ignition: coil and breaker points

Horsepower: 135 at 3,600 rpm

Torque: 253 at 1,800 rpm

A Rochester downdraft carburetor on a dual-plane intake topped the Rocket V-8. Crowning it was a side-entrance air cleaner.

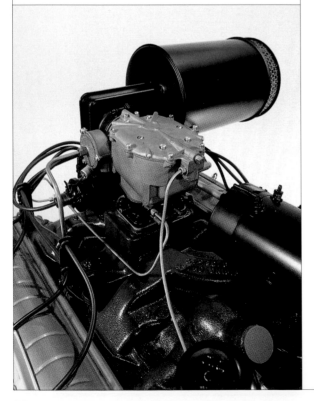

also could use a shorter, sturdier crankshaft. And with boring no longer so limited, increased cylinder diameters also translated into more room for bigger, wider valves—that is, if they were located overhead.

Long-stroke L-head V-8s could be dull luggers just like their inline counterparts. As was the case with any engine, overhead valves represented the best way to wake up a bent eight by, among other things, making breathing an easier chore. L-heads, by nature, didn't breathe all that well, as the air/fuel mixture and spent gases had to follow inhibited routes through upward-facing valves laid out beside the bores in the cylinder block. Contrarily, OHV heads allowed much smoother passages into and out of combustion chambers that were located fully atop the cylinders, a preferred position that enhanced volumetric efficiency through improved flame propagation.

And along with these more efficient chamber shapes came newfound compression levels. Increasing the squeeze applied to the air/fuel charge by the piston was long ago recognized as a sure-fire way to speed up the reciprocating process and thus make mucho horsepower. But compression levels were limited prior to the 1920s by fuel quality. Predetonation then was a problem, as too much compression would set off the charge before its appointed time, and too much compression early on equaled anything over 4:1 or so.

A solution to this problem came two-fold. First, Britain's Harry Ricardo, in 1922, successfully designed a squish-type combustion chamber that created turbulence in the air/fuel mixture as it was compressed. That turbulence greatly improved combustion efficiency and reduced the tendency for the fuel to predetonate due to inherent hot spots, such as around the exhaust valve. In turn, the Ricardo chamber allowed compression as high as 4.5:1, even with the existing bad gas.

Improved fuels represented the other half of the solution. In 1923, Charles "Boss" Kettering, the engineering genius who had fitted Cadillac with the industry's first electric self-starter in 1912, teamed up with the Ethyl Corporation's Thomas Midgley Jr. to create tetraethyl lead, an additive that greatly increased gasoline's octane rating. More octane was the main key to increasing compression, and reportedly 3 cubic centimeters of ethyl in a gallon of gas instantly bumped up a 55-octane rating by 15 points. Compression ratios jumped above the 6:1 level almost overnight. Octane continued rising, and Kettering's GM research team experimented further with high-compression engines. Immediately following World War II, they were playing with an OHV six with an amazing 12.5:1 compression running aviation-fuel-like 100-octane gasoline.

That work contributed greatly to Oldsmobile's development of the Rocket V-8, explaining why it initially was called the "Kettering engine." But Kettering's honored moniker already was tied to Cadillac, where John Gordon, Harry Barr, Ed Cole, and crew had been working on a modern short-stroke OHV V-8 since 1937. Olds officials wanted to avoid confusion between the two powerplants and thus changed the name. Some, like engineer Gilbert Burrell, wanted everyone to know that the Rocket V-8 was "strictly an Oldsmobile project." Cadillac people didn't exactly agree, and some even harbored just a little disdain for what they considered to be a copycat. When word got out in 1947 that the upcoming Olds V-8 would displace 303 cubic inches, Cole and Barr hustled back to their drawing boards to enlarge their developing V-8 from 309 cubes to 331, just to keep some distance between the two squabbling corporate cousins.

Led by Burrell, Olds engineers began preliminary work on the Rocket V-8 in 1946. Burrell's assistant was Elliott "Pete" Estes, who was leading Pontiac when the GTO was born. Before the Olds Rocket assignment, Estes had worked under Kettering on the aforementioned high-compression six-cylinder project. He and Burrell got approval for their design in October 1947, and the engine went into production in November 1948. Though similar in many ways to its Cadillac counterpart, the two shared no parts.

Cadillac's 160-horsepower, 331-ci V-8 debuted one month before Oldsmobile's 135-horse Rocket. Compression in the Caddie was 7.5:1, compared to 7.25:1 for the Olds. Either number was considered high back then, and even higher ratios lay ahead in the not-so-distant future, all thanks to Kettering's cutting-edge experiments. Some L-heads at the time featured comparable compression, but Oldsmobile engineers had already determined that 8:1 was as high as the side-valve engine could go. It was that limiting factor that had helped convince them to switch to overhead valves.

A downdraft carburetor on a dual-plane intake crowned the Olds V-8. That carb was a side-entrance type, as it was mated up to a long, cylindrical cross-flow air cleaner/silencer assembly that spanned the engine from valve cover to valve cover. And like the Cadillac V-8, the Rocket featured an intriguing design that made its trend-setting short stroke possible: slipper-style aluminum pistons, which were able to slip down low between the crankshaft's counterweights, thanks to radial cutouts on each side. Without the cutouts, piston skirts would have conflicted with the crank, meaning a longer stroke would have been required.

The Cadillac's stroke was 3.625 inches, its bore 3.8125 inches. Oldsmobile's 3.4375-inch stroke was paired up with a 3.65-inch bore. Compare those numbers with the retiring Olds straight eight's bore and stroke of 3.25 by 3.875 inches. Also note that the new Olds eight's crank measured only 25.4 inches long, compared to 38.875 inches for its L-head forerunner.

Once on the road, the two GM V-8s inspired various short-stroke, overhead-valve followers, including Chrysler's high-powered hemi-head V-8, introduced to rave reviews in 1951. Studebaker too joined the OHV V-8 fraternity that year, as did Ford in 1954 and Packard, Hudson, and Nash in 1955. In the General Motors club, Buick joined its fellow members in 1953, followed by Chevrolet and Pontiac two years later.

Back in 1949, Cadillac earned *Motor Trend* magazine's "Car of the Year" honors for its new V-8 models. Oldsmobile's Rocket 88, meanwhile, was showcased as the prestigious pace car for that year's Indianapolis 500. But with its industry-leading power-to-weight ratio, the Rocket 88 did more than look good for a lap or two on a racing oval; it also became the first big star on Bill France's new National Association for Stock Car Racing circuit.

Oldsmobiles won six of the nine races held during NASCAR's inaugural Grand National season in 1949 and followed that up with 10 of 19 the next year. Racing glory also came south of the border, where Herschel McGriff and Ray Elliott drove a Rocket 88 to victory in 1950 in the first Carrera Panamericana, the grueling event better known as the "Mexican Road Race."

Though more NASCAR wins came in 1951 and 1952, Oldsmobile's on-track adventures were soon eclipsed by those of Hudson, a company that stuck with the good ol' L-head, demonstrating that the overhead-valve V-8 hadn't completely taken over in Detroit—but just give it a couple of years.

Originally introduced in 1949 for Oldsmobile's big, plush 98 line, the division's V-8 really took off when dropped between the lighter 76 models' fenders, resulting in the truly hot Rocket 88. Shown here is a 1950 Rocket 88 Holiday coupe.

The big oil-bath air cleaner atop this 1950 Rocket V-8 was an option that year. A conventional dry-element filter was standard.

Hudson's Twin H-Power six-cylinder engine was hot on its own when introduced for 1952. But company engineers just couldn't leave well enough alone; they also put together the 7X package, which, among other things, added an overbored block, a high-lift cam, and a high-compression head held down by studs drilled into the block.

CHAPTER 11

Round and Round in a Step-Down:
Hudson Twin H-Power Straight Six

Modified prewar Fords did the bulk of the running around in circles when Bill France opened the National Association for Stock Car Racing for business in 1948. But NASCAR's founding father envisioned a more modern image for his fledgling competition circuit,  so in 1949 he originated a special series for relatively new, Strictly Stock models.

Hudson Hornets dominated NASCAR racing from 1951 through 1954. Herb Thomas won the driver's title in 1951 and then finished second in this Hornet the following year to Tim Flock, another Hudson pilot.

NASCAR's first Strictly Stock event was a 10-mile exhibition held in south Florida in February 1949. This was followed by NASCAR's first official Grand National race, held in June at a 3/4-mile dirt track in Charlotte, North Carolina. A '49 Lincoln won that 150-miler, but Oldsmobile's newfangled 88 quickly took center stage on the Strictly Stock circuit. Olds was NASCAR's first Grand National manufacturer champ, as well as its second and third.

And though Oldsmobile officials still could brag about their cars winning the most NASCAR races in 1951, it was Herb Thomas who copped top driver honors that year in his *Fabulous Hudson Hornet*. Totaling 13 wins in all in 1951, Hudson ranked second behind Oldsmobile's 20 victories while kick-starting a stock-car dynasty that soon had racing people forgetting all about the Rocket-powered Olds. Hudsons took a whopping 27 checkered flags in 1952, with Tim Flock's Hornet scoring the most seasonal points, followed closely by Thomas' familiar No. 92 sedan. Thomas then won 12 races on his own to take home the Grand National points championship in 1953, as Hudson domination continued rolling on. Counting all races run in all stock car circuits—NASCAR and American Automobile Association (AAA)—Hudsons won 49 times in 1952, 46 more in 1953. Another 18 victories followed in 1954 before the company's fortunes (both at the home office and the track) went on the wane. Lee Petty's Chrysler narrowly nudged out Thomas' Hornet for the Grand National points title in 1954, which was the last year for the so-called "Step-Down" Hudson.

Inspiring that nickname was a design that laid the foundation for Hudson's historic NASCAR successes. Introduced in 1948, Hudson's first truly new postwar model featured trend-setting slab-side styling on the outside, supported beneath by a monobilt skeleton. This unitized layout featured box-steel girders that were welded into a single unit to tie the body and frame together as rigidly as anything ever seen from Detroit. Along with being super strong, the frame also featured widely spaced perimeter rails that ran outside of the rear wheels, thus giving the car a skirted look in back. This wide spacing allowed the interior compartment floor to drop low between those rails, meaning passengers had to step down when entering—thus the name.

That low floor also meant the roofline could be dropped without reducing head room, resulting in a car that was as long, low, and sleek as anything then on American roads. Or American tracks. The performance potential of Hudson's rigid, sure-footed, relatively aerodynamic Step-Down models quickly became clear, especially to professional hot-foots like Herb Thomas, Marshall Teague, and Tim Flock. In those days, winning NASCAR races had as much to do with simply surviving as it did with running the fastest, and Strictly Stock cars didn't come any more durable than the Step-Down Hornet.

That's not to say, however, that those fabulous Hornets didn't carry some sting beneath their hoods. Sure, Hudson didn't rely on overhead valves during the early-1950s like Oldsmobile, or even a V-8. But its reliable inline six-cylinder still packed a punch. Introduced at a healthy 262 cubic inches in 1948, this brawny L-head was, in Hudson's words, "the most powerful mass-produced six built today." It was 24 percent larger than the six it replaced, it featured four main bearings instead of the previous engine's three, and it was the first Hudson powerplant to use full-pressure lubrication. Output was 121 horsepower, only 5 ponies less than Hudson's 254-ci straight eight. Many critics claimed Hudson's smaller (by cylinder count) engine was a better choice than its eight-cylinder brethren in 1948. According to *Mechanix Illustrated*'s Tom McCahill, "In the six-cylinder class, there isn't a car in the country that will out-perform the Hudson six."

Helping spur on Hudson's rapid rise to NASCAR fame in 1951 was an even more formidable motor. By increasing bore (from 3.56 inches to 3.81) and stroke (from 4.38 inches to 4.50), Hudson engineers produced the largest, most powerful L-head six ever. Displacement was 308 cubic inches (5 more than the Olds V-8), and horsepower was 145. Compression was 7.2:1, a decent squeeze for the day, certainly so for an L-head.

Like its surroundings, Hudson's 308-ci straight six was as tough as a battleship, beginning with its bulletproof cylinder block. Company engineers had left conventional cast iron behind in 1932 in favor of a modern high-chrome alloy that was harder than hard, and it was this Superman-type strength that at least partially explained how this old-fashioned engine managed to stand so tall in a highly competitive postwar world full of cutting-edge V-8s. According to brochures, the 308 six's "extreme ruggedness" made it a natural competitor: "The oversize bearings, the extreme rigidity and hardness of the block, the weight and stiffness of the crankshaft—in fact, the extra sturdiness built into all parts—make it possible to utilize extra power."

Helping make it possible for Herb Thomas's Hornet to win with relative ease was none other than ace racing mechanic Henry "Smokey" Yunick, long-time proprietor of Daytona Beach's "best damn garage in town," and the same man who would later in the decade work

Herb Thomas on the way to victory in his *Fabulous Hudson Hornet* at Atlanta's Lakewood Speedway in July 1953. Thomas copped 12 wins that year while capturing the NASCAR Grand National championship.

Hudson's bulletproof 308-cubic-inch L-head six-cylinder was well-suited for the tortures of stock car racing. Adding Twin H-Power enhanced the engine's advantages even further.

This special split exhaust header was just one of many race-ready components offered through Hudson's Severe Usage parts pipeline.

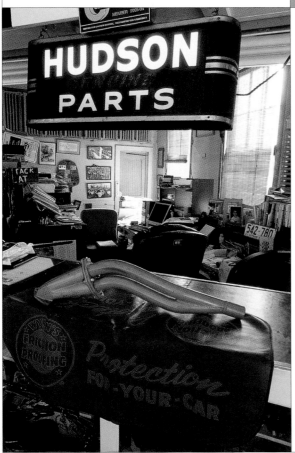

similar competition-minded magic for Chevrolet and Pontiac. Yunick's main man at Hudson in the race-winning days of the early 1950s was a young engineer named Vince Piggins, who himself would end up working for Chevrolet once Hudson faded from the scene. At Chevrolet, Piggins went on to oversee the division's performance parts development projects and was the main man responsible for the Z/28 Camaro's debut in 1967. He also was responsible for the various exotic COPO cars, the most prominent being the all-aluminum 1969 ZL-1 Camaro.

At Hudson in 1952, Piggins was put in charge of the company's severe-usage parts program, a direct response to the rigorous—make that torturous—challenges presented by NASCAR racing. The promotional opportunities that stock car competition offered had not been lost on company officials, explaining their willingness to create such a narrowly focused program. In a September 1952 meeting, Hudson parts merchandising manager H. L. Templin was among the first to speak out about the relations between road and track, claiming that "the publicity covering Hudson's many wins has been of untold benefit to us." As much as Templin pressed for complete dealer familiarity with the company's severe usage parts project, it would for the most part remain a low-key operation. But it was a successful one.

Bill France's goal had always been to create a competition arena for stock cars. By officially opening its severe usage parts counter for business, Hudson made things completely legal per NASCAR mandates—these race-ready parts were available from the factory as stock parts, so they were completely legal for stock-car competition. Not since the record-setting Duesenbergs of the mid-1930s had a major American automaker involved itself so fully in a factory-backed high-speed project. And never before had such involvement also resulted in such a prominent performance enhancement passed on to the everyday driver.

That enhancement was "Twin H-Power," an optional dual-carburetor induction setup that helped boost the big six's output to 160 horsepower. According to Hudson's hype-masters, "The secret of the amazing results which Twin H-Power provides is that it so accurately measures gasoline, so evenly distributes it to each cylinder, and so thoroughly vaporizes the fuel with air that it provides what the engineers call far better 'breathing' and combustion than has heretofore been obtainable. Most important, this greatly improved efficiency is obtained on regular grade gasoline. There is no need to pay for premium grade fuels. (Twin H-Power) provides jetlike pickup and a sustained flow of terrific energy. (And it) gives you stepped-up power where you need it most, in the ordinary driving range."

At the same time, a whole host of stepped-up parts began trickling out of Piggins' department for not-so-ordinary driving ranges. Early NASCAR races had demonstrated that stock steel wheels were factory cars' weakest link, coming apart easily when stressed. And when racers reinforced their wheels themselves, spindles tended to break. Piggins' men responded by working with the Kelsey-Hayes Company to develop the industry's first heavy-duty, race-ready rim. Offered as well were spindles and steering arms that were shot-peened for extra strength. Beefy, large-diameter rear axles, strengthened hubs with bigger bolts, stiffer shock absorbers, dual exhaust kits, an extra-high-performance cam, a heavy-duty radiator, an extracapacity fuel tank, high-compression heads... the list was as impressive as it was long.

In 1953, Hudson also introduced the "7X" racing option for the 308 six-cylinder. Officially announced primarily as a short-block replacement engine package, the $385 7X engine featured an overbored block that was plunge cut into the cylinders to unshroud the valves. Inside went a high-lift cam, and a high-compression head went on top, held down by studs drilled into the block. Twin H-Power was included, as was a special split exhaust manifold. Common estimates put output for the 7X six-cylinder at 210 horsepower. Very few were sold.

In 1954, some of the tricks tried with the 7X package were extended to the regular production line. Hudson's six was fitted with a lumpier cam and an aluminum high-compression (7.5:1) head, which upped output to 160 horses, 170 with optional Twin H-Power. In terms of horsepower per cubic inch, the Twin H-Power Hudson in 1954 ranked right up at the top, along with Detroit's various OHV V-8s.

But that honor served as a suitable send-off for the fabulous Hornet, as the very last Step-Down Hudson rolled off the line at the company's old Jefferson Avenue plant in Detroit on October 29, 1954. Beginning in 1955, Hudsons became glorified Nash models built right alongside their corporate cousins in Kenosha, Wisconsin, after the two independents merged to form American Motors.

Within a year, racing people had forgotten all about Hudson, as Chrysler created its own dynasty in 1955 and 1956, this one powered by a hemi-head V-8.

Hudson's racing days ended when the old L-head six-cylinder and the Step-Down body were dropped after 1954. Here, a dusty 7X block rests alongside Hudson's new-for-1955 overhead-valve V-8 at the Ypsilanti Automotive Heritage Museum in Michigan, housed in a former Hudson dealership building.

1954 HUDSON TWIN H-POWER

Type: water-cooled inline six-cylinder L-head

Construction: cast-iron block with detachable head

Main bearings: four

Bore and stroke: 3.81x4.5 inches

Displacement: 308 cubic inches

Valves: two per cylinder

Lifters: solid

Compression: 7.5:1

Induction: two Carter two-barrel carburetors

Horsepower: 170 at 3,800 rpm

Torque: 278 at 2,600 rpm

Chevrolet introduced American drivers to fuel injection in 1957, offering its Ramjet option for both passenger cars and Corvettes. Passenger car applications ended in 1959; the last injected Corvette engine (shown here) appeared in 1965 with 375 horsepower.

CHAPTER 12

Shootin' the Juice: Chevrolet Fuel-Injected V-8

Chevrolet didn't call its all-new V-8-powered 1955 model the "Hot One" for

nothing. This baby not only looked the part, it

also could cook like blue blazes, thanks to 162

standard horsepower, 180 with the optional

four-barrel carburetor and dual exhausts.

1965 CHEVROLET L84 CORVETTE

Type: water-cooled 90-degree OHV small-block V-8

Construction: cast-iron block and heads

Main bearings: five

Bore and stroke: 4.00x3.25 inches

Displacement: 327 cubic inches

Valves: two per cylinder

Lifters: solid

Compression: 11:1

Induction: Ramjet fuel injection

Exhaust: dual mufflers and tailpipes

Horsepower: 375 at 6,200 rpm

Torque: 360 at 4,000 rpm

Chevrolet's new modern overhead-valve V-8 was a sensation when it appeared in 1955. Displacement was 265 cubic inches; maximum output was 180 horsepower. *David Kimble cutaway, courtesy General Motors*

"It certainly appears that a Chevrolet V-8 with (the) optional 180-bhp engine and 4.11 axle will out-accelerate any American car on the market today!" claimed a *Road & Track* review. *R&T* road test results were startling: 0-60 in 9.7 seconds, 17.2 ticks for the quarter-mile. Any American car running under 10 seconds from rest to 60 miles per hour represented big enough news in those days. That this factory hot rod was a Chevy—just a year departed from its yeoman Stovebolt existence—certainly represented grounds to use an exclamation point, maybe even two!!

As early as December 1951, General Motors' officials had begun planning a thoroughly modern makeover for Chevrolet, this even though the division already was firmly entrenched as Detroit's annual sales leader. Plain six-cylinder practicality—next-to-nothing more, certainly nothing less—had long been the main key to the Bowtie boys' success. But the annual runner-up, Ford, was modernizing fast, and word was soon out about Dearborn's development of a new overhead-valve V-8 to replace its old, antiquated flathead for 1954.

Not to be left resting on their laurels, GM execs in April 1952 moved up-and-coming Ed Cole over from Cadillac to become Chevrolet chief engineer. Another Cadillac man, Harry Barr, joined him. Both had played major roles in Cadillac's development of its short-stroke, overhead-valve V-8, and now they were tasked with working similar magic for the luxury line's lower-priced corporate cousin. The fruit of their labors, Chevy's so-called "small-block" V-8, remains running ever stronger today, more than a half-century after first making the scene.

Its overhead valves and unprecedented compactness (thus the small-block name) were two of the main attractions from the start. At 530 pounds, Chevrolet's 1955 V-8 was 42 pounds lighter than the venerable Stovebolt six that dated back, at least in essence, to 1929. As for power, the maximum advertised rating for Chevy's passenger car six in 1955 was 136 horsepower, compared to the aforementioned new V-8's 162 standard horses.

Impressive as well were the first small block's manufacturing processes, which were radically simplified. Most notable was a new casting technique that, among other things, required fewer sand cores. Compared to Cadillac's V-8, which needed 22 cores to create a block, the Chevrolet V-8 block was cast using only 9 major and 3 minor cores.

Keeping things simple and cost-effective were also among goals set during cylinder head development. For starters, one symmetrical casting worked for both right and left sides. And instead of using rocker arms all mounted together on a conventional central shaft, these heads featured lightweight stamped-steel rockers, each rocking independently on its own ball-pivot stud. Along with saving weight, this design also meant that deflection wouldn't be passed on from one arm to the others via that shaft. And it was simply easier to manufacture and thus cheaper than typical shaft-mounted arrangements. Finally, combined with Ed Cole's oh-so-short 3.00-inch stroke, those ball-stud rockers helped the new small block wind up like no other V-8 then on the market.

Few seem to remember that the ball-stud rocker idea actually came from Pontiac, which had been developing its own modern OHV V-8 since 1946. GM engineer Clayton Leach came up with the design in 1948, and his rockers were then implemented in the new Pontiac V-8 initially targeted to appear for 1953. But various delays pushed that debut back two years, and by then Ed Cole had copied the individual stamped-steel rocker design for his hot, new V-8.

Nearly all else about the first small block was of genuine Chevrolet design. Additional innovations included hollow pushrods that fed all-important lubricants to the engine's top end, doing away with the need for troublesome external lines or extra oil passages within the block.

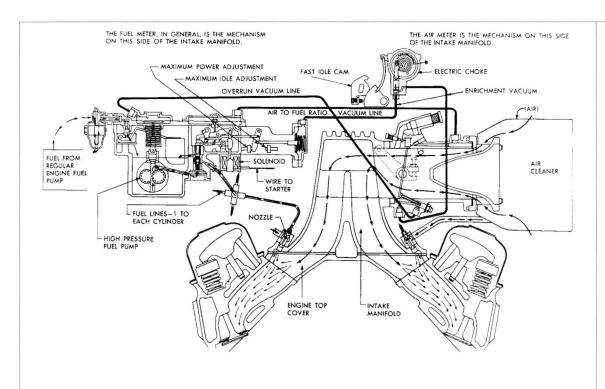

THE FUEL METER, IN GENERAL, IS THE MECHANISM ON THIS SIDE OF THE INTAKE MANIFOLD.

THE AIR METER IS THE MECHANISM ON THIS SIDE OF THE INTAKE MANIFOLD.

MAXIMUM POWER ADJUSTMENT
MAXIMUM IDLE ADJUSTMENT
OVERRUN VACUUM LINE
FAST IDLE CAM
ELECTRIC CHOKE
ENRICHMENT VACUUM
AIR TO FUEL RATIO VACUUM LINE
(AIR)
FUEL FROM REGULAR ENGINE FUEL PUMP
SOLENOID
WIRE TO STARTER
AIR CLEANER
FUEL LINES—1 TO EACH CYLINDER
NOZZLE
HIGH PRESSURE FUEL PUMP
ENGINE TOP COVER
INTAKE MANIFOLD

Chevrolet's Rochester-supplied "fuelie" equipment was of continuous-injection design, as opposed to direct-injection designs, which incorporated injectors into the combustion chambers. The Ramjet system shot fuel continuously into the airflow just before it entered the cylinder heads.

Up top was an intake manifold that also served as a cover for the valley formed between cylinder banks in the V configuration. Initial displacement was 265 cubic inches.

The 1955 Corvette also was treated to V-8 power, and this warmly welcomed addition helped save the fiberglass two-seater from an early death. Six cylinders (or even four) may have suited the European sporting crowd just fine back then, but they didn't exactly stir the souls of horsepower hounds on this side of the Atlantic. With a more aggressive cam, dual exhausts, and a Carter four-barrel carburetor, the Corvette's 265 V-8 pumped out 195 horsepower, which made for a real thrill ride. From there, "America's sports car" never looked back.

Corvette popularity truly took off in 1956, when a sexy new body and improved chassis joined the small-block V-8. New that year, too, were dual four-barrel carburetors, which boosted the 265 V-8's output to 225 horsepower. But that wasn't all. Zora Arkus-Duntov released his legendary solid-lifter camshaft in 1956, and the aptly nicknamed "Duntov cam" helped pump up maximum muscle to an unofficial 240 horsepower. Why unofficial? Because Chevrolet paperwork never posted an advertised number, in turn due to the fact that this "special high-lift camshaft" option was recommended "for racing purposes only."

The Corvette's future grew even brighter in 1957 as an optional four-speed stick debuted and Chevy's small block grew up further. First came 18 more cubic inches, as the 265 V-8 was bored out from 3.75 inches to 3.875. When topped by the dual-carb option, this 283 V-8 produced 270 horsepower in top trim. Yet once more, that wasn't all Zora Duntov and crew had up their sleeves.

Easily the most thrilling Chevy V-8 to date appeared for 1957, topped by "Ramjet" fuel injection, a Rochester-built performance option offered for all Chevrolet models that year. The Corvette's 283-cubic-inch "fuelie" small block was listed under RPO 579, while its passenger-line counterpart was identified as RPO 578. Two injected 283 V-8s debuted for 1957, one with 250 horsepower, the other with 283. The former used 9.5:1 compression and a hydraulic cam; the

Various injected V-8s were offered in 1957, including the competition-ready air box option, which added a cool-air induction system atop the 283-horsepower 283-cubic-inch V-8. Only 43 air box Corvettes were built.

Small-block cylinder heads featured individual stamped-steel rocker arms, a design Chevrolet engineers borrowed from their Pontiac counterparts. This lightweight valvetrain worked in concert with the small block's short stroke to help the Chevy V-8 wind out like nobody's business.

latter relied on the mechanical Duntov cam and 10.5:1 compression. An FI V-8 would last appear in Chevrolet's passenger-car ranks in 1959, while the fuel-injected Corvette rolled on until 1965.

Fuel injection represented a real sensation on the American market in 1957, but at the same time it was certainly nothing new on the world stage. Early fuel injection experiments date back to 1891, with the first working systems being tried by 1906. Inspiration for this work came from the fledgling aircraft industry, which needed a new way to feed airborne engines. Early carburetors were crude enough working on a flat plane, where they often starved out or flooded, depending on how much the fuel supply was sloshed about. Inject far more severe centrifugal forces, and even upside-down operation, into the equation, and the carburetor didn't mix well at all with aviation applications.

Injection systems for ground-based vehicles didn't come into vogue until diesel truck engines started proliferating in the 1920s. Diesel fuel injection was patented in 1926, and by 1930, Germany's Bosch company had become the leader in the field. The first truly successful FI application in the gasoline-powered, regular-production, automotive world came in 1954, when Mercedes-Benz made Bosch injection standard on its stunning 300SL gullwing coupe.

Inspired by the classic German machine, Ed Cole couldn't wait to apply similar technology to the Corvette. GM already had tried various FI experiments during the early 1950s, with Engineering's John Dolza doing the bulk of the work. Once the 300SL appeared, Dolza's efforts were accelerated, and then Cole put Zora Duntov on the project in 1955. A prototype fuel injection system was being tested on a Chevy V-8 by the end of the year, and not even a 1956 test track crash that put Duntov into a body cast could keep him from finalizing the design in time for its 1957 introduction. He was officially made head of Corvette development soon afterward.

Chevrolet's Ramjet injection option featured a two-piece cast-aluminum manifold, with the lower, valley-cover section incorporating tuned ram tubes running to the intake ports, while the upper casting created an intake plenum. Air and fuel metering mechanicals attached on opposite sides of this plenum. Precisely metered gasoline from a high-pressure fuel pump was injected continuously, through eight injectors, into the air flow just before it entered the cylinder heads. Thus, the Ramjet unit was of "continuous-injection" design. "Direct injection" involves mounting the injectors inside the combustion chambers. Continuous injection doesn't require nearly as much fuel delivery pressure as direct injection.

Ramjet injection did existing carburetors one better by, among other things, eliminating the flooding and fuel starvation caused when hard turns sent the gas supply in the carb bowl centrifuging off away from the pickup—a problem high-flying Corvette road racers knew well. And the Ramjet system not only delivered fuel more evenly in a much more efficient manner, it did so instantly. Throttle response was superb. In *Road & Track*'s words, "the fuel injection engine is an absolute jewel, quiet and remarkably docile when driven gently around town, yet instantly transformable into a roaring brute when pushed hard."

On the downside, fuelie Chevys earned an early reputation for hard starts and finicky operation. Uninformed owners didn't help matters during starting by typically pumping the accelerator, a definite no-no. And keeping everything in proper tune was a must, although that was difficult considering that so few local mechanics were qualified to tinker with fuel injection in 1957. Some frustrated fuelie owners even went so far as to replace the Ramjet system with conventional carburetors. Silly them.

Teething problems aside, the fuel-injected 283 V-8 helped put Corvette performance at the cutting edge in 1957. *Road & Track* testers managed a 0–60 run in 5.7 seconds—great numbers today, simply stunning for the 1950s. Quarter-mile times, at 14.3 seconds, were alarming too. Chevrolet officials were equally proud of the top FI V-8's output rating, claiming that the injected small block was Detroit's first engine to produce 1 horsepower per cubic inch of displacement. (Sorry, guys. Chrysler's 300B luxury performance car of 1956 could've been equipped with an optional 354-ci hemi-head V-8 rated at 355 horsepower. Do the math.)

Corvette buyers found various performance packages listed under RPO 579 in 1957. RPOs 579A and 579C both featured the 250-horsepower FI 283, with the letters "A" and "C" referring to the transmission choice—579A featured the four-speed manual, 579C the Powerglide automatic. RPO 579B was the designation assigned to the fabled 283-horsepower 283. The four-speed manual was the only transmission available behind the 283/283 V-8.

A fourth version of the 283-horsepower Corvette, RPO 579E, also was offered in 1957, this one clearly built with competition in mind. Known as the "air box" option, this package featured a special cool-air induction system. The idea was simple. A plenum box was mounted on the fender well panel on the driver's side. At the front, this box mated to an opening in the support bulkhead beside the radiator. Inside the box was an air filter. At the rear was a rubberized duct that ran from that filter to the Ramjet injection unit. Cooler outside air entered through the bulkhead opening into the box, then through the filter into the FI system. The result was the release of a few extra ponies on top end as the air box Corvette's injected 283 sucked in its denser supply of precious oxygen.

Additional air box modifications included moving the tachometer from its less-than-desirable stock spot in the center of the dash to atop the steering column. Both the radio and heater were deleted, and, with the former gone, ignition shielding wasn't required beneath the hood. This, in turn, meant plug wires could be run more directly from the distributor to the spark plugs over the valve covers as far away from the hot exhaust manifolds as possible. Plug wires on all other 1957 Corvettes were routed the long way down along the cylinder heads below the manifolds, because this was the easiest place to mount the static-suppressive shielding.

Priced at a whopping $726.30, RPO 579E cost about 50 percent more than the garden-variety 283/283 fuelie, leaving little wonder why so few were released. Only 43 air box Corvettes were built in 1957, bringing total fuel injection production that year to 1,040.

Various Ramjet updates appeared during its nine-year run, with the most noticeable being a switch from the original one-piece plenum to a low-profile two-piece unit for the 1963 Sting Ray. Early plenums featured ribbed tops, replaced in 1960 by a plain-top casting. The Sting Ray's plenum featured an attractive bolt-on lid that incorporated both fins and Chevy's familiar crossed flags.

Maximum output increased, too, to 290 horsepower in 1958, 315 in 1961, and 360 in 1962, the first year for the Corvette's enlarged 327-cubic-inch small block. That same 360-horse 327 fuelie (then known as RPO L84) represented the top power option for the new Sting Ray in 1963; then L84 output reached its zenith the following year at 375 horsepower. Save for the exotic air box package, the fuelie option was priced the same, $484.20, from 1957 to 1962. That figure had jumped to $538 by the time the last L84 was planted within fiberglass fenders in 1965. Production peaked in 1963, when 2,610 L84 Corvettes were built.

Explaining the fuelie Corvette's demise was simple: why spend so much for 375 small-block horses when the new 396-cube big-block delivered 425 horsepower for about half the cost? Chevrolet sold 2,157 L78 big-block Sting Rays for 1965, compared to a mere 771 of those last injected L84 models. Little did disinterested Corvette buyers then know that fuel injection would later become the only option beneath forward-hinged hoods.

Basically a fuelie V-8 with a carburetor in place of the Ramjet injection system, the L76 327 V-8 was a popular Corvette option in 1963, offering 340 horsepower at considerably less cost compared with its 360-horsepower L84 cousin.

Bright ignition shielding was familiar to Corvette customers for many years, being required to keep radios inside the cars static-free. Conventional steel bodies suppress this interference; fiberglass shells don't. Here, a 1965 L84's shielding is removed to expose the distributor normally hidden within.

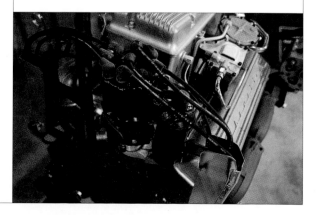

Looking more like an airplane engine than an automotive power source, the Corvair's Turbo-Air "pancake" six-cylinder was the brainchild of Ed Cole, the same engineering genius who helped bring Chevrolet's small-block V-8 to life. The alternator on this 1964 Corvair six is a nonstock owner-preferred piece.

CHAPTER 13

A Breath of Fresh Air: Chevrolet Corvair Six-Cylinder

Most Americans with a minimal knowledge of automotive lore and legend

know at least some of the story behind Chevrolet's Corvair, the small car

that, along with Ford's Falcon and Plymouth's

Valiant, kicked off this country's compact

craze in 1960.

Two Rochester one-barrel carburetors fed the standard Turbo-Air six-cylinder engine. Below each carb was an intake manifold cast integral with its cylinder head.

To recap, this bittersweet tale basically represented a case of bad timing, with a touch of bad judgment, bad luck, bad press, and bad politics thrown in for good measure.

If Lee Iacocca hadn't invented the pony car... if Ed Cole's R&D guys had just spent a little more time (make that money) ironing out the rear suspension... if the grapevine hadn't done such a complete job of overblowing the things the R&D guys overlooked (or underfunded)... if a certain accident victim had been driving a Falcon instead of a Corvair when he was killed in California in 1960... if this same unfortunate teenage driver hadn't had a lawyer as a stepfather... if this gentleman's law partner hadn't set his sights on a career in auto accident damages litigation, with Corvair mishaps being his main focus... if Connecticut Senator Abraham Ribicoff hadn't decided to put a feather in his congressional cap at the expense of supposedly unsafe American cars like the alleged consumer-killing Chevy.

And if Ralph Nader had only grown up wanting to be a fireman. If, if, if...

Although initial deficiencies were soon fixed beneath Chevrolet's innovative compact and the car's name eventually cleared in court, the Corvair never quite recovered from its early troubles. Despite claims to the contrary, Chevy's rear-engine wonder was reasonably safe at most speeds, yet the public had made up its mind, as had GM officials, who as early as April 1965 already were spreading the word to cease any future development work on Cole's unconventional compact—this about six months before pioneering consumerist Nader's first big whistle-blowing work, *Unsafe at Any Speed*, was published. As it was, designers by then were busy developing GM's answer to Ford's wildly popular Mustang, and it was a foregone conclusion that the Camaro to come would more or less take the Corvair's place in Chevy's product pecking order. So it was that the last Corvair rolled off the line in May 1969. Plain and simple, this little breath of fresh air deserved a better fate.

After driving Chevrolet's all-new 1960 Corvair in the summer of 1959, *Sports Car Illustrated*'s Karl Ludvigsen called it "the most profoundly revolutionary car, within the framework of the U.S. automotive industry, ever offered by a major manufacturer." No, its cost-cutting compact nature wasn't necessarily what set it apart from anything seen before. Independents Crosley, Kaiser, Nash, and Hudson all had tried to introduce America to serious downsizing prior to the Corvair's debut, with home appliance king Powel Crosley's first efforts dating all the way back to the late-1930s. Imported minimachines too began infiltrating the U.S. market after World War II. Most prominently among the imports was by Volkswagen's Beetle, the pint-sized German that helped inspire the Corvair's rush to market, as well as its final design.

Revolutionary aspects of the Corvair's design included four-wheel independent suspension with traditional coil springs and parallel A-arms up front, nontraditional swing axles (with coils and trailing A-arms) in back. But most notable, of course, was the innovation that necessitated its independently sprung tail: the car's rear-mounted six-cylinder engine. Along with showing up in the space where Americans were accustomed to stowing their luggage, this powerplant also raised eyebrows with its layout. Nicknamed the "pancake six," the Corvair engine was of the flat, opposed layout most familiar to private pilots of small airplanes. And like the VW flat four, the Corvair six was air-cooled, this done primarily to reduce engine weight and (to a lesser degree) avoid the complicated plumbing required to water cool a rear-mounted engine.

As much as wags early on liked to call the Corvair the "Chevy-VW," the basic idea for its unfamiliar (from a Yankee perspective) layout began percolating in Ed Cole's active gray matter well before Volkswagen began gaining momentum in the U.S. market in the last half of the

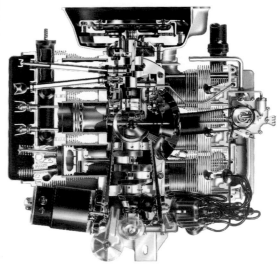

Left: The Corvair wasn't America's first rear-engine design, but it was the most successful. More than 62,000 were built during its first year (1960) on the road. The last rolled off the line in May 1969.

Above: Weight-saving aluminum was used throughout the Turbo-Air flat six. The six-finned cylinders were the only main components made of cast iron. Original output was 80 horsepower.

Below: The Corvair's unipack power team engine/transaxle package was mounted rather simply into the car as one piece from underneath.

1950s. As early as 1946, Cole, then a Cadillac engineer, was testing rear engine designs. He'd already learned about air cooling while working on military tank development during World War II, then put this concept into practice after being made manager of Cadillac's Cleveland tank works in 1950. The M-42 tank he built there featured an air-cooled, horizontally opposed six-cylinder engine supplied by Continental, a company also responsible for the smaller flat six in private pilot Cole's Bonanza plane.

In May 1952, GM's high-flying genius was made chief engineer at Chevrolet, and three years later came his greatest claim to fame, the "Hot One." But even as he was overseeing the creation of Chevy's new modern V-8, Cole also was directing his staff to "invent" an equally new small car powered by—you guessed it—an air-cooled opposed six-cylinder. A working prototype engine was running—in, of all things, a modified Porsche—by the spring of 1956, but the car itself was still little more than a drawing board concept. All that changed when Ed Cole became Chevrolet general manager in July 1956.

A complete prototype model was itself up and running in September 1957, just in time to get GM President Harlow Curtice's nod to go into production. GM's Board of Directors gave its final approval in January 1958. Eager automotive press members began getting their first looks at the finished product in August 1959, and what greeted them when they opened the lid in back was Chevrolet's 140-cubic-inch "Turbo-Air" flat six, initially rated at 80 horsepower.

Unfamiliar in essentially every respect, the Turbo-Air engine used weight-saving aluminum everywhere it could. The two-piece crankcase (split vertically down the crankshaft axis), cylinder heads, rear engine housing, clutch housing, and crankcase cover were all aluminum. The only major structural components cast out of iron were the six individual cylinders, which were

The hottest Corvair was the turbocharged Spyder, introduced in 1962. Shown here is the last Spyder, the 1964 model. The name was dropped, but optional turbocharging remained available to Corvair buyers through 1966.

A tale of two Corvair power packages: the 164-cubic-inch Turbo-Air engine in front produced 110 horsepower using two Rochester carburetors. Its turborcharged counterpart in back was rated at 150 horsepower.

appropriately finned per air-cooling practices. "Presenting a maximum of surface to the cooling air being passed over the engine, the fins help to conduct heat away from the combustion chamber and adjacent region," explained Chevrolet Engineering paperwork.

Cylinder heads too were finned on their combustion chamber sides to help keep things cool. Of a modified wedge design, these chambers were fitted with valve seat inserts (nickel steel for the intake valves, chromium steel for the exhausts) to save the aluminum structure from the pounding as the valves opened and closed. Each head also was cast with its own integral intake manifold, a clever bit of foundry work that complemented Cole's simple, weight-conscious ideal. Short steel sleeves were pressed into the exhaust ports on the head's opposite side, and additional fins were cast in between these sleeves to cool the ports as spent gases flowed through. Cast-iron exhaust manifolds clamped to those three sleeves on each side of the engine and directed hot gases into a Y-pipe that led to a single muffler located to the engine's right.

Cast-aluminum slipper-type pistons and forged-steel rods were bolted up to an exceptionally sturdy forged-steel crankshaft held in place by four main bearings. Compression was 8:1. Centrally located below the crank, the camshaft curiously featured only nine lobes: one for each of the six intake valves and three for their six exhaust counterparts. Each exhaust valve on one side shared a cam lobe with its opposite valve in the other head. Valve sizes were 1.340 inches on intake, 1.240 inches on exhaust. Tubular steel pushrods, 1.57:1 stud-mounted rockers, and hydraulic lifters completed the valvetrain. Cam specs were 0.360-inch lift, 232/252 (intake/exhaust) degrees of duration, and 28 degrees of overlap.

Two Rochester one-barrel carburetors bolted atop each integral intake/cylinder head handled induction chores. A balance tube connected both intakes to equalize vacuum pressure, which in turn translated into smoother operation at low speeds or idle. Hoses on top ran from the carburetors' throats to a central air cleaner.

Below that air cleaner, and hiding all of the Turbo-Air six from view, was a sheetmetal shroud that housed a large belt-driven blower on top. This shroud served as a plenum to contain cooling airflow, which was sucked in through a thermostatically controlled damper by an impeller spinning at 1.6 times crank speed. Along with forcing cooling breezes past all those fins, the blower also directed airflow to an oil cooler mounted at the left rear corner of the engine. From there, the forced flow exited through two openings in back.

A controversial aspect of the Turbo-Air's layout involved the belt that drove the blower. Like the fan belts on typical water-cooled engines, this flexible unit was driven off a crankshaft-mounted pulley, which of course rotated vertically. But the blower's impeller spun horizontally, meaning its drive belt had to turn a corner on top of the engine. This was achieved by adding parallel pulleys—mounted vertically but angled 90 degrees away from the crank's axis—into the route, bending the belt forward in the process. This process also twisted the belt more than might have been desirable, leading some early critics to wonder about premature failure. That problem did not arise, although some belts apparently were thrown at high speeds in 1960. Deepening pulley grooves solved this problem.

Turbo-Air enhancements included a lumpier cam that upped output to 95 horsepower for an optional pancake six offered in 1960. In 1961, stroke was increased from 3.38 inches to 3.44 (bore stayed at 2.6 inches), resulting in a displacement jump up to 145 cubic inches. Standard output remained at 80 horsepower, but top optional power was up to 98 horses, supplied by the aptly named "Super Turbo-Air" six.

Optional output increased again to 102 horsepower for 1962, but the really big news that year involved the introduction of the Corvair Spyder. Standard output for the Spyder was 150 horsepower, this leap made possible by turbocharging the Super Turbo-Air engine. Along with Oldsmobile's Jetfire coupe, the Spyder introduced exhaust-driven forced induction to the U.S. market that year, but both cars proved to be more icing than cake, and turbo engines didn't really make a mark in America until the 1980s.

Fed by a single Carter carburetor, the Spyder's turbo engine featured various modifications, including beefed-up reciprocating pieces and a lighter cooling fan. Compression, however, was kept at the original Turbo-Air's 8:1, compared to the Super Turbo-Air's 9:1 squeeze. Lower compression always goes hand in hand with forced induction, predictably due to the high pressures boosted into combustion chambers by either turbochargers or superchargers.

Calling the Spyder a "poor man's Porsche," *Car and Driver* reported 0–60 performance of 11.7 seconds for the turbocharged Corvair—nothing earth-shattering, mind you, but still exciting for a budget-conscious compact. Consider further that, in many minds, the Spyder represented an acquired taste—for those with refined tastes.

As Corvair proponent Karl Ludvigsen wrote in *Automobile Quarterly* in 1970, the Spyder featured "the first modern engine built and sold by Detroit that required a skilled, interested driver to extract the best performance from it. It was not designed down to the incompetence level of a theoretical average driver. Features like the Spyder engine made buying a Corvair feel like admittance to membership in an exclusive club."

Although the Spyder itself was history after 1964, Chevrolet continued offering a turbo option for the Corvair up through 1966. In 1964, the Turbo-Air six was enlarged further to 164 cubic inches after the stroke was stretched to 2.94 inches, yet advertised output for the turbo Spyder remained at 150 horsepower. That figure rose to 180 horsepower for 1965, the increase primarily due to improved airflow through the turbocharger.

Standard output for the Corvair's pancake six was up to 95 horsepower when the end of the line quietly came in May 1969. If only...

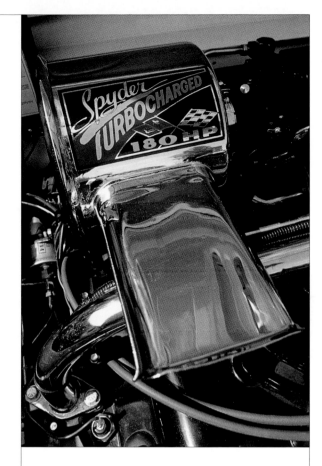

The decal on this 1964 Spyder should read 150 horsepower. The 180-horse turbo six didn't appear until 1965. Either way, the car was a blast to drive. *Car and Driver* called it a "poor man's Porsche."

Chevrolet's 409-cubic-inch W-head V-8 was already making big noise on America's drag strips when the Beach Boys began singing its praises in 1962. Offered in both single- and dual-carburetor forms during its short career, the 409 maxed out at 425 horsepower.

CHAPTER 14

So Fine: Chevrolet 409 V-8

Brian, Dennis, and Carl Wilson were still sticking baseball cards in their bicycle spokes when Chevrolet first made the hot car scene in 1955. A few years from stardom, as well as their driver's licenses, the Wilson brothers—60 percent of southern California's legendary Beach Boys—never thought twice about singing  the praises of Chevy's first modern overhead-valve V-8, especially since they had yet to think twice on singing about anything when the Hot One debuted.

1962 CHEVROLET 409

Type: water-cooled OHV 90-degree W-head V-8

Construction: cast-iron block and cylinder heads

Main bearings: five

Bore and stroke: 4.3125x3.5 inches

Displacement: 409 cubic inches

Valves: two per cylinder (2.19-inch intakes, 1.72-inch exhausts)

Camshaft: solid lifters (0.4396-inch lift)

Compression: 11:1

Induction: two Carter AFB four-barrel carburetors

Exhaust: cast-iron header-style manifold, dual mufflers and tailpipes

Horsepower: 409 at 6,000 rpm

Torque: 420 at 4,000 rpm

The W-head got its name due to its staggered valves, which traced out a W across the cylinder head's face. That face was basically flat, as the combustion chambers were formed within the bores.

No biggie, though, the first 265-powered Bel Air made enough noise on its own. And some say the echoes still can be heard more than a half-century down the road.

Almost overnight, Chevrolet had made driving fun for Average Joe and his friends. Serious horsepower for the masses—who'd-a thunk it? In place of the good ol' Stovebolts came cool rides that especially attracted the younger set, a soon-to-be-massive market segment that Detroit would be paying extreme attention to in only a few years. Okay, so maybe Chevrolet people didn't invent hot cars, nor were they necessarily first to take note of the rapidly growing youth market. But they certainly did a lot to bring the two together.

So did Brian Wilson. Possibly inspired by a white '61 Impala that, in February 1961, rolled defiantly into Pomona, California, for the National Hot Rod Association's Winternationals, Wilson (along with coauthor Brian Usher) penned the car song to end all car songs, "409," released by Capitol Records in May 1962. In truth, it was probably Usher who had more to do with the song's inspiration, as he owned a 409 Chevy at the time. But either way, the catchy tune helped rocket both the car and those bushy, bushy blonde balladeers into national prominence.

Actually, Chevrolet's 409-cubic-inch V-8 already had drawn its fair share of fanfare nationwide by the time American teens started getting all revved up over the Beach Boys and their first big hit. Veteran drag racer Don Nicholson had made some noise of his own 15 months before, showing up at Pomona in his aforementioned '61 Impala. Nicholson's appearance at the Winternationals represented the 409's public debut, and what a debut it was.

Official production of Chevrolet's 409 V-8 had begun the month before, when Nicholson received the first example off the line in a crate just three days prior to the big NHRA drag race meet. Hastily "dyno-tuned" and tested for stock-class competition, Nicholson's 409 left the Pontiac and Ford guys gawking after a 13.19-second trial pass topping out at 109.48 miles per hour, and then slammed the hammer down with a 13.59/105.88 Stock Eliminator victory over another '61 409. "Dyno" Don's 409 would go on to become a match race legend in 1961, touring the country and never once losing to a Ford. It was a fast start to a performance legacy that would run strong up through 1965.

The 409 tale dates back to 1958, when Chevrolet introduced its 348-cubic-inch V-8, often called a "W-head" because of the pattern made by its alternating valve positions. Look down on top of a 348 cylinder head and the valves trace out a "W," or an "M," depending on your relative position. Originally conceived with both car and truck duty in mind, the W-head was Chevrolet's first big-block V-8 and was the product of, among others, the engineering minds of Donald McPherson, Richard Keinath, Fred Frincke, Denny Davis, Cal Wade, and Al Kolbe. In the beginning, this group worked on two different size big-blocks, one displacing 307 cubes, the other 348. But once it was determined that the smaller version wouldn't be able to make any measurable power advances compared to the existing 283-ci small-block V-8, the 307 was dropped and all efforts were focused on the 348.

Along with its uniquely shaped valve covers, the 348 stood out from the crowd, thanks to its unconventional combustion chambers, which resided inside the cylinder bores, not in the heads as was customary. The working face of the 348 head was basically flat (valves opened and closed in slight pockets), while combustion chambers were created in the bores by sloping each cylinder bank's deck down on top at a 16-degree angle off perpendicular. This left a wedge-shaped squish area between piston and head at top dead center.

An idea basically borrowed from Mercedes by Al Kolbe, this design reportedly simplified head production and allowed the use of larger valves, the latter because of revised geometry.

The angled deck surfaces transformed the upper bore openings from circles into ellipses, which translated into increased cross-sectional bore area. More bore cross-section meant there was more room for larger-diameter valves. The 348's intake valves measured 1.94 inches across, 1.66 for exhausts; both measurements qualified as large for the time.

Other performance-enhancing features included staggered valves. Conventional V-8s at the time featured straight-line valve layouts because their rocker arms were mounted together on long shafts that ran the length of each head. GM's innovative ball-stud rocker arm, introduced by Chevrolet and Pontiac in 1955, allowed Chevy engineers to independently position valves where they would work best. In a 348 head, intake valves were positioned up high near the intake manifold runners. Exhaust valves, in turn, were found down close to the exhaust manifolds. This arrangement also translated into less passage wall area to inhibit intake and exhaust flow.

All 348s were high-compression (9.5:1 or better), all relied on at least a four-barrel carburetor (no single two-barrels; no way, no how), and all had dual exhausts. The ultimate 348 available during its four-year run from 1958 to 1961 was the Super Turbo-Thrust, which was fed by three Rochester two-barrels and used solid lifters in place of the tamer Turbo-Thrust's hydraulic units. Maximum advertised output was 350 horsepower.

The 348 existed as Chevrolet's hottest offering during its first three years and remained so early into 1961. But by then, the original W-head had evolved as far as it could. So it was, that late in 1960, engineers went back to the drawing board and re-emerged the next year with the 409. Although most considered the 409 a bored and stroked 348, it wasn't quite as simple as that.

For starters, boring the 348-ci cylinder block represented a risky proposition—not enough iron existed between the water jacket and cylinder bore. This fact forced engineers to recast the W-head's block, allowing the bore to increase from 4.125 inches to 4.3125. Stroke at the same time was stretched from 3.250 inches to 3.5, resulting in the new displacement figure that fit so well in the Wilson/Usher lyrics. More important was how well those 409 cubes matched up to Pontiac's 421, Ford's 406, and Chrysler's 413.

Modifications were plenty from there, so much so that swapping parts between the 348 and 409 basically was out of the question. New forged-aluminum pistons featured centered wrist pins and symmetrical valve reliefs milled straight across the piston top in pairs. Their 348 counterparts had offset wrist pins, one large intake relief, and one smaller exhaust relief, meaning a 348 required two opposite sets of four pistons, each set with its own part number. All 409 pistons interchanged regardless of which cylinder bank they were going into. Tying those pistons to a beefed-up forged-steel crank were shortened, reinforced connecting rods, while superior Morraine 500 steel-backed aluminum bearings replaced the 348's outdated Morraine 400 pieces.

Cylinder heads closely resembled the 348 design, but they were specially cast to accept larger-diameter pushrods and were machined on top for heavier valve springs. Valve sizes increased to 2.066 inches on intake, 1.720 on exhaust. Compression was 11.25:1.

At the heart of the 409 was one of the more radical stock-issue cams of the day. Lift, at 0.4396 inch, was up substantially in comparison to the 348, but it was the solid-lifter cam's long duration and healthy overlap that truly set it apart. Intake duration was 317 degrees, exhaust was 301, and total overlap came to 85, meaning the intake valve opened 59 degrees before top dead center (TDC), while the exhaust valve closed 26 degrees after TDC. Excessive overlap works wonders for high-rpm operation once inertia takes over and helps move things along, seemingly against physical laws. But heavy overlap is a bear to live with at idle or lower speeds, something a 409

Chevrolet engineers created the powerful W-head V-8 with truck applications in mind, as this 1960 Spartan Model 80 attests. The 409 V-8 also was offered as a heavy-duty truck option.

The famed 409 and flashy Super Sport Impala both were introduced early in 1961. Chevy's first SS was offered only with a W-head V-8, either the existing 348 or new 409.

IT FEELS GOOD, LOOKS BETTER and GOES GREAT!

Take any one of Chevy's five '61 Impalas, add either the new 409-cubic-inch V8 or the 348-cubic-inch job and a four-speed floor-mounted stick, wrap the whole thing in special trim that sets it apart from any other car on the street, and man, you have an Impala Super Sport! Every detail of this new Chevrolet package is custom made for young men on the move. This is the kind of car that Chevy insiders mean when they say Chevy, the kind that can only be appreciated by a man who understands, wants, and won't settle for less than REAL driving excitement.

Here are the ingredients of the Impala Super Sport kit: • Special Super Sport trim, inside and out • Instrument Panel Pad • Special wheel covers • Power brakes and power steering • Choice of five power teams: 305 hp. with 4-speed Synchro-Mesh or heavy-duty Powerglide, 340 hp. with 4-speed only, 350 hp. with 4-speed only, 360 hp. with 4-speed only • Heavy-duty springs and shocks • Sintered metallic brake linings • 7,000-RPM Tach • 8.00 x 14 narrow band whitewalls • Chevrolet Division of General Motors, Detroit 2, Michigan.

*Optional at extra cost, as a complete kit only.

MAY, 1961

Above: Header-style exhaust manifolds helped the 409 breathe easy.

Above, center: Only one 409 was offered in 1961: a 360-horsepower version fed by one four-barrel carburetor. A dual-carb 409, rated at 409 horse-power, appeared in 1962.

Above, right: The W-head's staggered valve layout is demonstrated (below left of the distributor in back) in this cutaway.

owner quickly discovered in 1961. As *Motor Trend* explained, "Although the (409) will idle at 750 rpm, it will not pull smoothly under 1,500 and is 'happiest' when operated over 2,000 rpm."

Happily feeding hefty gulps of air/fuel mixture to the 409 was a large Carter AFB carburetor on an aluminum intake. Foregoing the 348's triple-carb setup, engineers turned to a single carburetor that basically matched the 348's trio in flow and met NASCAR's mandate that labeled multiple-carb arrangements illegal for stock car racing. From there, a Delco-Remy ignition, featuring a dual-breaker, centrifugal-advance distributor, sparked the mixture, and low-restriction, header-style exhaust manifolds hauled away byproducts.

The sum of these parts equaled 360 horsepower for Chevrolet's first 409, which mandated the installation of a four-speed manual transmission and a 3.36:1 rear axle when ordered as a midyear option in 1961. Also new on the options list that year was the Super Sport kit, introduced shortly after the 409 appeared, basically to showcase the king of the W-heads.

Various hot parts and dress-up pieces were part of Chevrolet's first SS package, beginning with triblade spinner wheel covers on the outside. In the inside was a padded dashboard, a Corvette-type grab bar atop the glove box opening, and a 7,000-rpm tachometer mounted on the steering column. Underneath went limited production option (LPO) number 1108, the police handling package, which added a stiffer sway bar up front, sintered-metallic brake linings, and heavy-duty springs and shocks all around. Power steering and brakes and 8.00x14 narrow-band whitewall tires were included too.

Overall, the 409 SS Impala looked and played the part of a truly hot car as well as anything Detroit had to offer in 1961. Rest to 60 miles per hour took only seven seconds or so, and the metallic brakes were an able match for that power. Wrapping things up was an image that screamed "cool" every bit as loud as the exhaust notes backing up the Beach Boys on their big 1962 hit.

Advertised output jumped to 380 horsepower in 1962, and an even more potent 409 joined the lineup, this one fed by two Carter four-barrel carbs. Rated at 409 horsepower its first year, this beast then soared to 425 horses for 1963 and 1964. Output for the single-carb 409 reached 400 horsepower in 1963 and stayed there up through 1965. Yet another variety, the "police option" 409, appeared in 1963, featuring a relatively mild hydraulic lifter cam, a softer 10:1 air/fuel squeeze, and an optional Powerglide automatic transmission. Listed under RPO L33, this civilized

409 was rated at "only" 340 horsepower. But anyone who thought this cooled-down W-head a sissy had another think coming: *Car Life*'s testers recorded 0–60 in 6.6 seconds and a top speed of 124 miles per hour for the L33 Chevy.

Only the 340-horse L33 and 400-horse L31 409 V-8s carried over into 1965 before the legendary legacy was superseded midyear by Chevrolet's new 396-cubic-inch Mk. IV big-block V-8. Total 409 V-8 production that last year was 2,828. Previous tallies were 8,864 for 1964, 16,902 for 1963, 15,019 for 1962, and a mere 142 for 1961.

Mightiest of this short-lived breed was the race-only Z11 rendition, created late in 1962 for Super Stock drag racing. Thanks to an increased stroke (3.65 inches), the Z11 actually displaced 427 cubic inches. Among its various features were special raised-port heads, an equally special intake created to match those large ports, and 13:1 compression. Advertised output was a token 430 horsepower, but many feel the actual figure was more like 530. Chevrolet also offered weight-saving aluminum body components to accompany the Z11 V-8 on the drag strip.

More than 50 Z11 Chevrolets were built from late 1962 into early the next year before GM officials sent down their infamous antiracing memo in January 1963. The corporation's top execs had seen enough of what supposedly had been banned by the Automobile Manufacturers Association in 1957. Both Chevrolet and Pontiac were heavily involved in racing during the late 1950s and early 1960s, despite the AMA edict against such shenanigans, and damned proud of it. Not so after January 1963.

Down the tubes, almost overnight, went Zora Duntov's Grand Sport Corvettes, Pontiac's big Super Duty Catalinas, and Chevrolet's Z11. Fortunately, the latter's alter ego stuck around on the street a little longer until its last appearance on the hit parade in 1965.

The supreme W-head was the race-only Z11, a 427-cubic-inch variant built in small numbers in 1962 and 1963. Special raised-port cylinder heads required the use of an equally special two-piece intake manifold. Z11 output was a token 430 horsepower.

Chevy's 409 V-8 was installed in various full-sized models (including a few four-doors) from 1961 to 1965. Shown here is a 409-powered 1964 Impala Super Sport.

The 340-horse police-option 409 appeared in 1963 crowned by a single four-barrel carburetor. It was offered again in 1964 (shown here) and 1965.

Carroll Shelby put the High-Performance 289 V-8 to good use between the fenders of his GT350 Mustang variant, introduced in 1965. Shown here is a 1966 Shelby Mustang small block, which relied on tri-Y headers to help pump out 306 horsepower.

CHAPTER 15

Wonder from Windsor: Ford High-Performance 289 V-8

Lee Iacocca and the rest of Dearborn's Better Idea gang knew they had themselves a hot-to-trot sensation even before Ford's first Mustang started kicking up its hooves on April 17, 1964. Initial beancounter forecasts claimed about 100,000 pony cars would sell that first year, but Iacocca knew better.

1966 SHELBY GT-350

Type: water-cooled OHV 90-degree High-Performance 289 V-8

Construction: cast-iron block and cylinder heads

Main bearings: five, with two-bolt caps

Bore and stroke: 4.00x2.87 inches

Displacement: 289 cubic inches

Valves: two per cylinder

Camshaft: solid lifters

Compression: 10.5:1

Induction: 715-cfm Holley four-barrel carburetor on an aluminum intake manifold

Exhaust: Shelby Tri-Y headers, dual mufflers and tailpipes

Horsepower: 306 at 6,000 rpm

Torque: 329 at 4,200 rpm

Ford's first Windsor small-block V-8 displaced 221 cubic inches in 1962. It was bored out to 260 cubic inches early that year, and this engine went into Shelby's original Cobra.

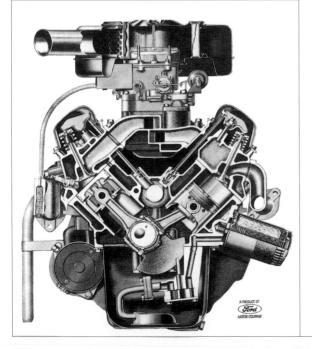

His battle cry became "417 by 4-17," the plan being to sell at least 417,000 Mustangs by April 17, 1965, breaking Detroit's record for "rookie" model sales in the process. No problem—more than 418,000 Mustangs hit the streets by April 17, 1965.

Perhaps the main key to the original pony car's unprecedented success involved what Iacocca called "the three faces of Mustang." First, was its affordable, economical side—the base six-cylinder model that possessed a sporty flair thanks to its carefree facade and standard bucket seats with floor shifter. If a buyer shelled out for all available comfort and convenience options, he or she drove away in what Iacocca saw as a mini-T-bird. Last, but certainly not least, was the Mustang's muscular personality, enhanced by optional V-8 power backed up by a four-speed stick. Some witnesses in 1964 even felt there were more identities hiding in there. According to *Car Life*, the first Mustang was "a sports car, a gran turismo car, an economy car, a personal car, a rally car, a sprint car, a race car, a suburban car, and even a luxury car."

That race car reference was a stretch, certainly at first, as truly hot performance was a bit slow in coming. Along with its standard 101-horsepower six-cylinder, the original Mustang offered only two rather mild "Windsor" small-block V-8s in April 1964, one rated at 164 horsepower, the other at 210. The former V-8 displaced 260 cubic inches and was fed by a two-barrel carburetor. The latter, displacing 289 cubes, featured a four-barrel carb.

Built in Ford's Windsor (thus the name) engine plant, these two small blocks traced their roots back only to 1962, the year Ford introduced its first midsized model, the Fairlane. Plans had called for the new Fairlane to offer both six- and eight-cylinder power, but Dearborn didn't have a suitable V-8 for the downsized platform. The hefty FE-series big-block, introduced four years before, simply wouldn't do, and the venerable Y-block V-8—which finally had replaced Henry's tired, old flathead in 1954—was too heavy for Ford's all-new intermediate.

Using the thin-wall casting technique developed to produce a lightweight six-cylinder for Ford's first compact, the 1960 Falcon, engineers created a new small-block V-8 that overnight superseded the Y-block in automotive ranks. As the name implied, the thin-wall technique involved ultraprecise casting processes that allowed engineers to minimize cylinder block wall thicknesses. Even more unwanted iron was cast aside by not repeating the extended-skirt design used by the Y-block. Unlike the Y-block's cylinder block, which dropped down well below the crankshaft, the Windsor block typically ended right at the crank's centerline and did so without sacrificing lower end durability.

When introduced for the 1962 Fairlane, the first Windsor small block relied on a bore of 3.50 inches and a stroke of 2.87 to equal a tidy 221 cubic inches—the same as Ford's history-making L-head V-8 of 1932. Advertised output was a measly 143 horsepower, a figure that surpassed Dearborn's strongest six-cylinder at the time by only 5 horses, explaining why this wimpy V-8 survived only into 1963. Midway through 1962, the Windsor block was bored out to 3.80 inches, resulting in the bigger, stronger 260 V-8 that served as a Mustang option in 1964. Meanwhile, testament to this small block's performance potential was made by Carroll Shelby, who began stuffing 260s into his aluminum-bodied AC Cobra in 1962.

After building 75 260 Cobras, Shelby was able to inject even more venom into his hybrid hot rod a year later, after Ford engineers increased the Windsor bore further to 4.00 inches, creating the popular 289 V-8. Introduced midyear in 1963, the first 289 was rated at 195 horsepower with a two-barrel carburetor shooting the juice. Shelby's men, on the other hand, were able to pull nearly 400 horses from the 289 for racing applications by, among other things, adding headers, a lumpy solid-lifter cam, sky-high 11.5:1 compression, and four Weber carbs.

Fairlane customers that year were treated to their own hopped-up Windsor V-8, this one fed by a single four-barrel carburetor. Nowhere near as radical as Shelby's concoction, yet still a force to be reckoned with, this midyear option was called the "High Performance" 289, and for

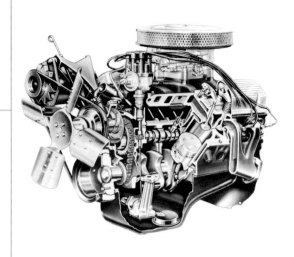

'64 Fairlane Sports Coupe; It can wear a Cobra kit, too!

Above: The Windsor small block was bored out to 289 cubic inches early in 1963. Standard output was 195 horsepower. Topped by a low-restriction air cleaner, the Hi-Po 289 produced 271 horses.

Left: The High-Performance 289 V-8 became a Fairlane option in mid-1963. Output was 271 horses, but that figure could be boosted up to as much as 343 horsepower by way of various "Cobra kits," created by Carroll Shelby's crew in California.

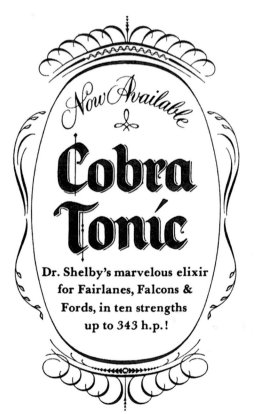

good reason. At 271 horsepower, it instantly transformed Ford's midsized models into what Ford promotional people called "the Cobra's cousin." As 1964 ads explained it, "Tie this savage little winder to a four-speed floor shift, tuck it into Fairlane's no-fat body shell, and you've got a going-handling combo that's mighty hard to beat ... and we mean that both ways!" Ford continued offering the "Hi-Po" 289 as a Fairlane option up through 1965, though these "going-handling combos" never did gain the fame achieved by their pony car counterparts.

The Mustang's third face was further enhanced in June 1964, when the Hi-Po 289 joined the pony car's extracost lineup, priced at $328, making it the breed's most expensive option. Though 271 horses didn't look like much, especially compared to Ford's 427 FE, which was then making 425 horsepower, they represented more than enough muscle to make a wild pony out of the Mustang. Brute force wasn't the aim anyway; high-winding capability was.

To this end, the Hi-Po 289 (identified with a "K" engine code) was carefully created from top to bottom to deal with high rpm without complaints. Its block featured strengthened main bearing caps (fastened down by two bolts, not four) holding a nodular-iron crankshaft, some of which were randomly inspected during assembly for metallurgic content. Cast-aluminum pistons were tied to that crank by beefed rods with reinforced big ends clamped down by large 3/8-inch bolts. Helping keep a K-code small block revving smoothly was a larger harmonic crankshaft balancer measuring 1 13/16 inches thick, as opposed to the standard 1-inch-thick balancer.

Durable valvetrain pieces included stiffer dual valve springs and hardened pushrods, spring retainers, and keepers. Screw-in studs (as opposed to the press-in pieces used in standard 289s) held cast rocker arms in place, and additional rev-conscious components included a larger pulley

Ford's High-Performance 289 V-8 became a Mustang option in June 1964, and this badge appeared on pony car flanks up through 1967.

A mean and nasty road racer in 1965, the GT350 was tamed a bit for 1966 to attract more customers. But the potent 306-horse Windsor small block remained.

(3.875 inches, compared to 2.75 inches) for alternator-equipped Hi-Po 289s and a special, stronger fan with increased pitch to maximize cooling capabilities. Like all 1964 Ford V-8s, the first K-code 289 used a generator. Alternators came along when 1965 production commenced.

Feeding the Hi-Po was a 600-cfm Autolite four-barrel on a standard 289 cast-iron intake. The cam was a solid-lifter unit with 0.457-inch lift, while the distributor was a dual-point type with mechanical advance. Special free-flowing exhaust manifolds helped speed spent gases along, and topping things off was a chromed, open-element air cleaner, a low-restriction piece that looked great and worked fine. Or did it look fine and work great?

Included in the K-code deal was the special handling package (quicker steering and stiffer springs, shocks, and sway bar) and Red Band tires. Though a mundane three-speed manual was standard behind the Hi-Po, a four-speed option was available. An optional automatic didn't appear for the Hi-Po until 1966, when Ford's far-from-politically-correct ads proclaimed that, "here, at last, is a memorable high-performance machine that you're not afraid to let your wife drive to the supermarket!"

Car Life's critics, meanwhile, didn't let one sexist quip slip while they lauded the 271-horse Mustang for its "obvious superiority to the more mundane, everyday Mustang." *Car Life*'s report continued, "Where the latter has a style and a flair of design that promises a road-hugging sort of performance, and then falls slightly short of this self-established goal, the HP Mustang backs up its looks in spades." Zero-to-60 mile-per-hour performance (with optional 3.89:1 gears) was listed at 8.3 seconds, 15.9 clicks for the quarter-mile. Armed with 4.11:1 gears, *Hot Rod*'s test subject lowered the 0–60 time to 6.9 seconds and did the quarter-mile in 15.5 seconds.

The Hi-Po 289 remained the Mustang's top performance option through 1966. It carried over briefly into 1967, but by then was overshadowed by the 390 GT big-block V-8. K-code 289 production for those three years was 7,273 in 1964–1965, 5,469 in 1966, and only 472 in 1967.

High Performance 289s also found homes in Carroll Shelby's GT-350 Mustangs from 1965 to 1967. These Windsor small blocks were rated at 306 horsepower, thanks to the addition of a 715-cfm Holley four-barrel on an aluminum intake and Tri-Y headers on the exhaust end. Cast-aluminum "Cobra" valve covers and a matching-style oversized oil pan completed the package.

The Hi-Po V-8 didn't return in 1968, which was the last year for the 289. A stroked (to 3.00 inches) Windsor was released concurrently for 1968, and then completely superseded its smaller brethren the following year. An even larger small block, the 351 Windsor, appeared for 1969 after engineers raised the existing cylinder block's deck height by 1.275 inches to allow room for more stroke, 3.50 inches in this case.

Both V-8s, the 302 and 351, survived up into the 1990s with the former morphing into its more familiar 5.0 form to again make the Mustang a formidable force on the street. Small-block Mustangs gained more muscle each year during the 1980s, and the 5-liter legacy truly emerged after carburetors were replaced by electronic fuel injection in 1987. The redesigned Mustang GT for 1994 retained the popular 5.0-liter V-8, but this veteran pushrod mill finally was retired the following year, replaced in 1996 by the 4.6-liter overhead-cam V-8.

Above, right: Hi-Po modifications included a larger crank pulley to better deal with higher rpm levels. A special fan was also used to aid cooling.

Right: A 715-cfm Holley four-barrel carburetor fed the GT350's Hi-Po 289. Typical 271-horse Mustang V-8s relied on a 600-cfm Autolite four-barrel.

Chrysler's 426 Hemi V-8 dominated American streets from 1966 to 1971. Nearly 11,000 of these dual-carb engines, all rated at 425 horsepower, went into Dodge and Plymouth muscle cars during that span.

CHAPTER 16

Haulin' Ass: Chrysler Corporation's 426 Hemi V-8

Four-twenty-six Hemi. Even the most casual of car nuts will nod respectfully

upon hearing these four words. Those truly in the know might go so far as

to bow in reverence. Indeed, even today,

30-odd years after its day in the sun,

Chrysler's 426-cubic-inch Hemi V-8 still

commands a loyal following. Make that

seriously loyal.

1968 DODGE/PLYMOUTH HEMI

Type: water-cooled OHV 90-degree V-8

Construction: cast-iron block and cylinder heads; hemispherical combustion chambers with inclined valves and centrally located spark plugs

Main bearings: five, with four-bolt caps

Bore and stroke: 4.25x3.75 inches

Displacement: 426 cubic inches

Valves: two per cylinder, activated by rocker arms mounted on parallel shafts

Camshaft: solid lifters

Compression: 10.25:1

Induction: two Carter four-barrel carburetors

Horsepower: 425 at 5,000 rpm

Torque: 490 at 4,500 rpm

Chrysler's original hemi-head V-8 debuted in 1951 and remained on the scene until 1959. Notice the twin rocker shafts and canted valves.

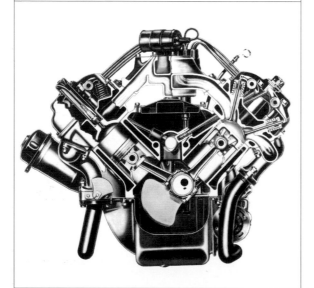

And whenever one of the rare Hemi cars built between 1964 and 1971 goes up for sale, it commands some seriously royal cash. Counting the race-ready versions of 1964 and 1965, Dodge and Plymouth rolled out roughly 10,500 Hemis during that eight-year run, and that supply has never been able to satisfy the ever-growing demand for such high-powered pieces of Mopar muscle history.

What's so hot about a Hemi? Just ask any SS Chevelle or Cobra Jet Ford owner who dared cross paths with one back in the 1960s. Chrysler officials weren't fibbing when they said this high-performance hunk of iron produced 425 horsepower. Well, actually they were, but only to protect themselves. Even the radical "race Hemi" of 1964–1965 was tagged with that same laughable rating, which, as engineer Tom Hoover later explained to no one's surprise, "was purely an advertising number." He continued, "Most of the (later) street Hemis would make 500 horsepower or better." In his opinion, using the 425-horse tag "was purely a matter of everybody being in fear that they would be called to Washington to testify before some committee that would say, 'You dirty dogs are out there making more power for cars and that's the un-American thing to do.' We were really worried about that as far back as the early 1960s. We were scared to death."

So too was the competition. Even when wrapped in a big, heavy Dodge Coronet or Plymouth Satellite body shell, the Hemi could produce 14-second blasts down the all-important quarter-mile, and that was with full exhausts plugging things up and wimpy street tires doing the rolling. Sticky slicks, unfettered tubular headers, and a few other tricks could easily put any Hemi Mopar into the 13-second bracket, if not into the 12s. Plain and simply put, brute force was this bad big-block's forte.

And it not only ran like hell, it also looked as mean and nasty as any production power-plant ever built. As if that huge air cleaner wasn't intimidating enough, there were those two dark, sinister-looking valve covers to further hike up the hairs on the back of your neck. Was this monster wrenched up in Detroit or stitched together in some mad scientist's lab? Like the bolts sticking out of Frankenstein's neck, those eight spark plug wires protruding from the middle of both of the big valve covers represented an eerie sight, if not downright alien.

That this muscle-bound mill appeared as unusual as it did was the direct result of its unusual design. Beneath those valve covers were cylinder heads featuring hemispherical-shaped "Hemi" combustion chambers. While the 426 Hemi was purpose-built from top to bottom to beat anything else on the street, it was that head construction that represented the main key to its success.

Hemi-head advantages were many. The symmetrical, domed combustion chambers, with their centrally located spark plugs, offered superb volumetric efficiency, and the physical nature of the rounded chamber allowed more room for bigger valves compared to typical wedge-head designs. And because those valves were inclined in opposite directions to match the curve of the hemispherical chamber, they allowed straighter, less restrictive passage for both intake and exhaust flow. Hemi ports didn't bend as much as those in a wedge head. The intake valves angled up to match their corresponding ports, and the exhaust valves pointed down to the same effect. In with the good air, out with the bad was simply a breeze for the free-breathing Hemi.

Downsides to the design included its relatively complex valvetrain and definitely excessive weight. Twin rocker shafts were needed to locate the inclined valves, as were different sized pushrods and rocker arms—exhausts and intakes did not match. Hemi heads also were extremely large, making for a tight fit between most fenders, be they on a big car or small. All that extra

mass translated into unwanted pounds; these hefty heads weighed as much as 25 percent more than comparable wedge-type units. This weight penalty, coupled with all the fuss and muss required to engineer and construct a pair of Hemi heads, had helped convince Chrysler officials a decade before to give up on the idea the first time around.

No, the 426 Hemi was nothing new. Dating back to development work originally considered in 1935, Chrysler's first hemi-head engine, the 331-cubic-inch Firepower V-8, had debuted in 1951. Before that, the basic design can be traced as far back as 1904, with later renditions coming in various World War I aircraft, sporting machines from Duesenberg and Stutz, racers from Miller and Offenhauser, and Jaguar's XK120 of 1949. But to that point, no automaker, foreign or domestic, had used the hemi head as effectively—and in mass production to boot—as Chrysler did beginning in the early 1950s.

Hemi power helped the third member of the Big Three unseat Cadillac atop Detroit's burgeoning horsepower race as the new decade dawned. At 180 horsepower, the first Firepower V-8 was 20 horses hotter than Caddy's best, making Chrysler the talk of the town in 1951. "The tremendous power of this V-8 is enough in itself to be a strong selling point," claimed a *Road & Track* review. "Regardless of the rest of the car's advantages or disadvantages, when you touch that throttle, you know something mighty impressive is happening under the hood." *Motor Trend*'s staff was so impressed that they awarded their "Car of the Year" trophy to the 1951 Firepower Chrysler. According to *Motor Trend*'s Griffith Borgeson, the hemi-powered Chrysler represented "a major step ahead in American automotive history."

Hemi-head technology appeared beneath DeSoto hoods in 1952 and then made its way into Dodge ranks the following year. In 1955, a special version of the Firepower V-8 became the first mainstream American engine to reach the 300-horse plateau. This particular engine was showcased in an equally special model, the C-300, the first of Chrysler's high-powered letter-series luxury hot rods and a car many old-timers like to call Detroit's first muscle car. According to *Mechanix Illustrated*'s Tom McCahill, the C-300 was "a hard-boiled, magnificent piece of semicompetition transportation, built for the real automotive connoisseur."

Semicompetition? The lavish and powerful 300s dominated stock car racing in 1955 and 1956 before retiring to a more civilized existence. Chrysler's beautiful brute kept on rolling strong with maximum horsepower hitting 390 in 1957. But then the big, heavy Hemi was dropped after 1958 in favor of lighter, equally powerful wedge-head V-8s that were easier and cheaper to build. The last 300 letter car was built in 1965.

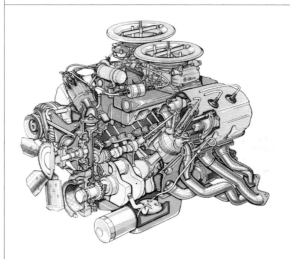

1965 CHRYSLER CORPORATION HEMISPHERICAL-COMBUSTION CHAMBER, ACCELERATION ENGINE

That fabled nickname was inspired by combustion chamber shape, which was hemispherical.

Centrally located spark plugs were also key to the Hemi's success. But with those plugs buried deep down in the center of each valve cover, long extensions were required to allow plug wires to make contact.

By then, the basic hemi-head concept had returned, although comparing the original Firepower V-8 with the newer rendition ran far beyond pairing apples with oranges. Based on Chrysler's 426-cubic-inch wedge V-8, the '64 Hemi was a competition-conscious engine never meant for the street. Its head-cracking high compression alone (12.5:1) made that fact apparent in a hurry. In December 1962, Tom Hoover had been asked to build a second-generation hemi-head V-8 intended only to promote Chrysler power at the track. Hoover's team then completed the job just in time for the sixth running of NASCAR's Daytona 500 in February 1964.

Per NASCAR rules, the new race Hemi was fitted with a single four-barrel carburetor in place of the dual fours used on the Firepower V-8s beneath 300 letter-car hoods. Race Hemi V-8s intended for drag strip duty sported twin four-barrels on Chrysler's cross-ram intake. Either way, as mentioned, the reported output rating was 425 horsepower, a joke to say the least.

Save for the Chrysler contingent, no one was laughing after the race Hemi hit Daytona in 1964. Hemi cars finished 1-2-3, with Richard Petty's winning Plymouth leading five other Mopars in the top 10. Petty went on to take the NASCAR seasonal championship by a margin so wide that rules moguls stepped in and banned the Hemi in 1965 because it wasn't a "regular-production engine." Chrysler's response was a boycott of the 1965 NASCAR season, which then allowed Ford to rule the roost. Dual-carb race Hemis, meanwhile, continued their winning ways at the drag strip in 1965.

Not ready to give up so easily, Chrysler officials in 1966 transformed the race Hemi into the street Hemi, a viable regular-production option that satisfied NASCAR's homologation requirements, allowing Dodge and Plymouth back into the stock car wars. Now the big 426 was unbeatable both on and off the track, though more than a little detuning was needed to take the Hemi to the streets.

Most noticeable was a major compression cut to a still-healthy 10.5:1. A less radical cam was stuffed in (although mechanical lifters remained) and cast-iron manifolds replaced the steel-tube headers. On top, a heated aluminum intake manifold mounting two 650-cfm Carter four-barrels superseded the exotic cross ram. Much of the race Hemi's stout foundation carried over, as did that same token output rating. The sum of these parts had the automotive press raving just as they had in 1951.

"If you missed the San Francisco earthquake, reserve your seat here for a repeat performance," began *Car and Driver*'s first review of the street Hemi, in this case a Plymouth. "Forget about your GTOs and your hot Fords—if you want to be boss on your block, rush down to your nearest Plymouth (or Dodge) dealer and place your order for a hemispherical combustion chamber 426 V-8. This automobile is the most powerful sedan ever, bar none."

It wasn't long before the 426 Hemi was being squeezed between the fenders of almost everything Dodge and Plymouth built, including a few four-door sedans. Belvedere, Satellite, Coronet, and Charger were the first to feel the joy in 1966. GTX, Super Bee, and Road Runner renditions quickly followed, as did the purpose-built Charger Daytona (along with its Charger 500 predecessor) and Plymouth Superbird in 1969 and 1970, respectively. But the biggest news came when the optional Hemi went into the lighter E-bodies, Plymouth's 'Cuda and Dodge's Challenger, in 1970. Although Hemi power had clandestinely found its way into some A-body Barracudas and Darts the previous year, those cobbled-together creations were intended primarily to go racing. The Hemi-powered pony cars of 1970–1971, on the other hand, went right into public hands to prove it to Boss Mustangs, Ram Air Pontiacs, and SS 454 Chevelles.

While the bodies varied on the outside, few changes were made to the street Hemi itself during its all-too-short six-year run. Dual inline carbs and that 425-horse tag carried over each year. Updates in 1968 included a hotter cam, revised valvetrain, and a windage tray inside a six-quart oil pan. Among other developments were hydraulic lifters, which replaced the maintenance-intensive solid tappets in 1970.

Of course, all that Hemi muscle didn't come cheap. The 426 engine alone cost about $800. Throw in a long list of mandatory heavy-duty options, and a Hemi car's bottom line took off as quickly as the machine itself. That formidable price tag, combined with a gnarly nature that didn't mix well at all with everyday use, helped make the Hemi a slow seller right up until it was last offered as a Dodge and Plymouth option in 1971. Hence the original short supply and the increasing demand during the decades since.

Say "Hemi for sale" today, and you'd better get out of the way.

Clockwise from above right: Dual four-barrel carburetors were standard fare atop the Street Hemi throughout its short, happy career.

Plymouth's new Hemi 'Cuda was equipped with the dramatic Shaker hood, named for the way that big scoop moved whenever the hammer went down.

The 426 Hemi was last offered beneath Mopar hoods in 1971. This Dodge Charger Super Bee was one of only 22 built that year with the 425-horse Hemi.

Pontiac's overhead-cam six-cylinder wasn't America's first OHC engine, but it was the first to make the mainstream in notable numbers. Standard output for the original 230-cubic-inch "Cammer," introduced in 1966, was 165 horsepower.

CHAPTER 17

When Less Was More:

Pontiac Overhead-Cam Six-Cylinder

History commonly overlooks the fact that Chevrolet wasn't the only

General Motors division to introduce a

modern overhead-valve V-8 in 1955.

Corporate cousin Pontiac too turned the

trick that year, and actually had its OHV

V-8 in development first.

Pontiac offered its OHC six-cylinder beneath Tempest/ LeMans and Firebird hoods through 1969.

Pontiac engineers also regularly fail to get credit for originally designing the ball-stud rocker arms so crucial to the Bowtie small block's success. Yes, Ed Cole's guys at Chevy did borrow this idea and then ran with it like scalded cats. An overnight sensation, Cole's "Hot One" brought buyers dashing into Chevy showrooms like dealers were offering free doughnuts or something. At the same time, Pontiac's new V-8 was helping turn things around in a big way for the company best known before for building cars your grandpa liked to drive, yet few grandkids today seem to remember this notable transformation.

Proven-yet-archaic L-head power, in both eight- and six-cylinder forms, had been the main attraction at Pontiac prior to 1955. Both of these old reliable inline engines were then dropped, and it was flashy V-8s only until 1961, when the division introduced its compact Tempest with its innovative rope-shaft drive and rear transaxle. Standard Tempest power came from a similarly curious concoction, a budget-conscious inline four-cylinder created by more or less sawing a V-8 in half down the crankshaft axis. Chrysler, in those days, had its slant six; Pontiac had a slant four, and did so up through 1963.

In 1964, the Tempest graduated in size as designers rolled GM's new A-body intermediate platform beneath it. Larger and predictably heavier, the midsized '64 Tempest needed more than four standard cylinders to haul itself around, and thus created a need to reinstate a six to the Pontiac powertrain team. Chief Engineer John DeLorean's group had been busy working on just such a project but wasn't anywhere near ready to put it into production when the A-body Tempest started rolling off the line. So this time it was Pontiac's turn to borrow a few things from Chevrolet—six cylinders.

Though assembled at Pontiac using some Pontiac parts, the '64 Tempest's standard 215-ci OHV straight six was basically a Chevy in disguise. Fed by a single one-barrel carburetor and designed to run forever, however yeomanlike, this straight-shooter doled out 140 yawning horses in such dull, durable fashion that even Pontiac engineers weren't ashamed about proclaiming its cream-vanilla nature. It was no wonder, then, that only about 25 percent of Tempest buyers in 1964 stuck with the standard six, the rest choosing to step up to the optional 326-ci V-8. The Chevy-sourced six-cylinder returned for a ho-hum encore in 1965 before a true Pontiac six finally arrived the following year.

True Pontiac was right. By 1966, the formerly conservative GM division had become well known for its pizzazz, this after introducing, among other things, its muscle-minded GTO in 1964, its prestigious Grand Prix in 1962, its award-winning Wide Track line in 1959, and its fuel-injected Bonneville convertible in 1957. And when the '66 Tempest appeared with a new standard engine, this just wasn't another garden-variety six meant only to help bring Grandma's groceries home. GM had never before built anything like it, a plain fact that DeLorean wasn't above bragging about, calling his creation "the newest and most exciting engine development ever to be offered by our divisions." Some in Detroit even felt Pontiac's newly appointed general manager was being humble. "He could have just as well extended his remarks to include the whole industry," wrote *Motor Trend* technical editor John Ethridge.

The object of DeLorean's affections—Pontiac's new 230-ci single-overhead-cam six-cylinder—was certainly an innovative approach to performance, at least in American terms. Europeans, of course, were, by 1966, well versed in the merits of the OHC six, with Jaguar's twin-cam rendition representing one of the more glamorous examples. Yankees weren't exactly strangers to the concept, witness the OHC six Fred Tone designed for the 1925 Wills Sainte Claire, built (however briefly) in Marysville, Michigan. No U.S.-born OHC engine of any cylinder count, however, had

ever appeared in great numbers before Pontiac's "Cammer" came along, making this America's first mass-produced overhead-cam engine.

Various innovative approaches also helped Pontiac's OHC six stand out. First and foremost was its cam-drive system, which used a fiberglass-reinforced rubber belt instead of a chain or gears. First seen on Germany's Glas 1-liter four-cylinder in 1961, this Gilmer belt didn't make much noise like a chain and also didn't require lubrication, the latter fact meaning it could be located outside of the engine block structure, which in turn represented a serious servicing plus. An easily removed die-cast aluminum housing, working in concert with a sheetmetal plate in back, kept the belt winding around in a clean environment for longer life.

Although the Glas firm recommended replacing its timing belts every 25,000 miles, Pontiac people were convinced that durability wasn't much of a concern. According to veteran engineer Malcolm McKellar, not one failure occurred during belt testing, not even after 100,000 miles worth of use. McKellar's crew also had tested a more conventional steel-reinforced belt, but found the fiberglass unit far tougher. Corrosion was a risk with the former, as was fatigue stress (caused by the repeated bending of the steel strands) after only about 50,000 miles. Excellent elasticity, combined with exceptional tensile strength, made the fiberglass belt a far better choice, proven by piles of miles of trouble-free operation. Pontiac's Gilmer belt featured 98 teeth and weighed 9.5 ounces. It was 49 inches long and 1 inch wide.

Controlling tension on that belt involved another neat little trick. On the passenger-side of the block was a die-cast aluminum housing that served as a mounting point for the distributor, oil pump, oil filter, and fuel pump. Inside the housing was a vertical shaft that spun both the

The OHC six's single camshaft was mounted inside the engine's attractive cast-aluminum valve cover. Hydraulically adjusted cam-following fingers activated the valves.

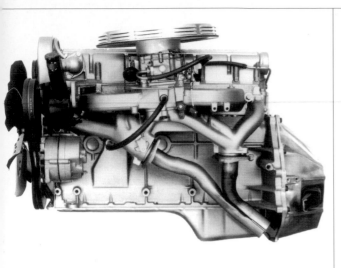

Adding a four-barrel carburetor and a split exhaust manifold (leading to dual exhausts) transformed the OHC six into its Sprint alter ego, which initially produced 207 horsepower. Maximum Sprint six output hit 230 horses before all was said and done.

distributor on top and oil pump below by way of a bevel gear that contacted a corresponding cog on a horizontal shaft that ran forward, ending in a sprocket driven by the timing belt at crankshaft speed. That horizontal shaft also incorporated an eccentric cam lobe that worked the fuel pump's diaphragm arm. This entire setup—shafts, pumps, housing, and all—could be moved vertically (thanks to slotted bolt holes) on a slanted mounting pad on the block, with this motion correspondingly moving the sprocket up front diagonally to tighten or loosen the timing belt. Talk about killing a bunch of birds with one stone.

Yet, as innovative as the timing belt and accessory drive setup appeared, it was McKellar's opinion that the cleverest aspect of Pontiac's OHC six appeared on top. Activating the valves were typical cam-following fingers that pivoted on not-so-typical hydraulic adjusters instead of simple pedestals with pesky screw adjusters. Other OHC engines required regular servicing to keep valve lash set at zero by way of such screws. But the Pontiac six automatically adjusted the clearance between valve stems and cam followers with its own oil pressure, a feature that McKellar claimed was key to making the Cammer work. American buyers would've never put up with the hassle of making valvetrain adjustments every 20,000 miles or so.

As for the camshaft in Pontiac's overhead-cam engine, it was cleverly mounted within seven bearings held in place inside the die-cast aluminum cover that looked so damn good on top of everything. Simply removing this cover brought the cam right along with it, making for another servicing convenience. This particular aspect proved important once troubles with cam wear started surfacing. Keeping ample oil pumping up to the top of the OHC six represented the design's only troublesome facet, and minding oil changes religiously was highly recommended to prevent sludge from inhibiting that much-needed flow even further. Drivers who let their OHC Pontiac's oil get thick were in trouble; those who kept theirs squeaky clean stood a good chance of putting this problem off.

That gremlin aside, the cam-on-top position did expectedly cut down on power-robbing reciprocating weight. Valvetrain inertia dropped by 27 percent compared to the Chevrolet six, and these savings translated into much higher rev limits. Pontiac engineers also inclined the valves a rather-steep 15 degrees toward their ports, a touch that aided breathing by reducing the bend encountered as the air/fuel mixture made its way into the combustion chambers. Valve inclination on the Chevy six had been 9 degrees.

Valve sizes in Pontiac's OHC six were healthy, certainly for a six-cylinder: 1.92-inch intakes, 1.60 exhausts. Cam specs were 0.400 inch of lift, 228 degrees duration. Both the intake and exhaust manifolds were mounted on the same side (driver's), and that intake mounted a one-barrel Rochester carburetor. Compression was 9:1. Advertised output was 165 horsepower. This package was listed as the standard power source for the Tempest and its upscale LeMans running mate in 1966 and 1967, as well as the F-body Firebird introduced for 1967.

A second, truly exciting OHC Pontiac six-cylinder also appeared in 1966. Called the Sprint, this sexy six produced 207 horsepower thanks to various additions, the most noticeable being a Rochester Quadrajet four-barrel carburetor topped by a chromed air cleaner similar to that found on Pontiac's GTO. Beneath the "Q-Jet" was a cast-iron intake manifold featuring tuned individual runners for each intake port. Additional modifications included a compression boost to 10.5:1 and the inclusion of spidery split manifolds on the exhaust end to allow for dual mufflers and tailpipes. A more aggressive cam (0.438-inch lift, 244 degrees duration) went on top, as did higher-rate dual valve springs.

The sporty Firebird Sprint debuted in 1967 with standard OHC power. Shown here is a 1968 Sprint convertible.

Along with this hopped-up six, the Sprint package for midsized Pontiacs in 1966 also included a Hurst-shifted three-speed manual transmission and a beefed-up suspension. A four-speed stick could've been added for a few more bucks. A similar Sprint option appeared as well for the Firebird when it made the scene the following year. In either platform, the OHC Sprint six-cylinder impressed the critics with the way in which it combined zippy performance and simple practicality.

"The Sprint-packaged Tempest will outperform most cars, which is remarkable for any six-cylinder these days," raved John Etheridge. His January 1966 *Motor Trend* report announced 0–60 in 9.2 seconds, the quarter-mile in 16.7 clicks.

"From the moment it takes over from the starter, you know there's something different about this engine," echoed *Road & Track*. "A throaty, entertaining exhaust note raps at you and is reminiscent of earlier single-exhaust Jaguar XKs. Like the Jaguars, it idles without any fuss at 600 rpm and runs without mechanical clatter at any speed up to 6,000. What this all means, really, is that for the first time since the days of the Hudson Hornet, an American six-cylinder car is news in the performance department."

The Firebird Sprint inspired similar compliments in 1967. Like its Tempest/LeMans companion, this Euro-style machine remained in production up through 1969. A stroke job (from 3.25 inches to 3.52, to go along with the 3.875-inch bore) the previous year had boosted displacement to 250 cubic inches, bringing output up along with it; the base OHC six now produced 175 horsepower, the Sprint 215. A third rendition for manual-transmission models was released for 1969, fitted with an even lumpier cam. This "high output" OHC six was rated at 230 horsepower.

Standard beneath a 1968 Firebird Sprint's hood was a 215-horsepower 250-cubic-inch overhead-cam six-cylinder. Compression was 10.5:1.

But after 1969, it was back to the conventional Chevrolet six-cylinder for Pontiac. Plain and simply, the OHC six was no cheapie on the supply end, and demand never had materialized like DeLorean had hoped. Even though the Sprints could outperform most entry-level V-8s, it was still the latter engines that ruled the streets back in the 1960s, regardless of what magazine road test results proved. Most buyers then were sure that bigger always had to be better. Though those attitudes would soon change after gas prices began soaring in the 1970s, it was too late for Pontiac's overhead-cam six, an engine that proved too soon that less could be more.

Ford's 335-horsepower 428 Cobra Jet V-8 was offered to Mustang buyers from April 1968 through 1970. The optional Shaker hood scoop appearing here debuted in 1969.

CHAPTER 18

Street Fighter: Ford 428 Cobra Jet V-8

Ford was king of the international racing world in June 1966, after winning

at Le Mans, the first time an American team had taken top honors at France's

fabled 24-hour endurance event. Dearborn-sponsored racers had taken command

back home the year before, as Jim Clark's

Lotus-Ford ended the Offenhauser dynasty at

the Brickyard in Indianapolis, and more

familiar Blue Oval models copped 48 of 55

races on NASCAR speedways.

Type: water-cooled 90-degree OHV FE-series V-8

Construction: cast-iron block and cylinder heads

Main bearings: five

Bore and stroke: 4.13x3.98 inches

Displacement: 428 cubic inches

Valves: two per cylinder

Camshaft: hydraulic (0.481-inch lift intake, 0.490-inch exhaust)

Compression: 10.6:1

Induction: 735-cfm Holley four-barrel carburetor

Horsepower: 335 at 5,400 rpm

Torque: 440 at 3,400 rpm

The king of the FE-series big blocks was the fabled 427 V-8, introduced in mid-1963 for both Ford and Mercury models. The single-carb 427 produced 410 horsepower; its dual-carb brother was rated at 425 horses.

USAC, SCCA, NHRA, whatever the initials, if it involved racing in the mid-1960s, it involved Ford, known since 1963 as the "Total Performance" company.

But not so fast...though Total Performance did translate into total domination at the track during the first half of the 1960, it was a totally different story on Main Street USA. The Ford faithful here at home in 1966 couldn't help but notice all those GTOs, SS 396 Chevelles, and Hemi Mopars leaving the supposed high-performance Ford rides in the dust. At the time, Dearborn simply had nothing to offer in the way of muscle for the masses like Pontiac and Chevrolet did in their big-block, midsized machines. While Ford's Fairlane GT, introduced in 1966, did feature reasonably potent big-block power, its 390-ci V-8 was no match for Pontiac's 400 or Chevy's 396.

Much the same could've been said when the Mustang's engine bay was enlarged for 1967 to make room for the popular pony car's first big-block. That optional V-8 was again the 390 GT with its underachieving 320 horses, which General Motors' two new big-block pony cars, the Pontiac Firebird 400 and Chevrolet SS 396 Camaro, had little problem running away from.

Help, however, was on the way. On April 1, 1968, Ford introduced its street performance savior, a car powered by a better idea first envisioned not within the firm's engineering halls but by an outside source. Or two. Inspiration for the 428 Cobra Jet V-8 initially came from an East Coast Ford dealer, with a little help supplied by a fast-thinking automotive journalist working clear across the country in California.

Robert F. Tasca Sr.—Bob to many, the "Bopper" to some—was Ford's most successful dealer in the 1960s. Tasca Ford, founded in November 1953 at 777 Taunton Avenue in East Providence, Rhode Island, had grown so fast that Dearborn officials just had to ask the main man how his relatively small dealership could move so many cars. Tasca kept no secrets and was soon advising Ford execs on the ways things should be done. It was then only a matter of time before his influence reached clear up to Henry Ford II's office.

Tasca early on had recognized that hot cars represented the latest going thing, so in 1961, he organized a special high-performance division (with Dean Gregson as its manager) to promote Ford power, both on the street and at the drag strip. His dealership began sponsoring its first drag car the next year, then put together its own race team late in 1962, after which time the motto around Tasca Ford quickly became "win on Sunday, sell on Monday." As long as Fords were winners, so too was Bob Tasca's dealership. Then again, when they didn't win ...

As Tasca later told *Super Stock* magazine in 1968, "We did well from '63 to '65, when the car-buying market was a young one. (Then) younger people (became) disenchanted with Ford's performance on the street and stopped buying." Ford's dwindling presence in Detroit's burgeoning muscle car race left Tasca and his men distraught, to say the least, even more so once the new big-block Mustangs started rolling off trucks in the fall of 1966. "We found the car so noncompetitive, we began to feel we were cheating the customer," explained Dean Gregson to *Hot Rod* magazine in late 1967. So they decided to take matters into their own hands.

Their solution came about almost by chance after a Tasca man over-revved the 390 in a '67 Mustang GT coupe. Instead of simply replacing the blown FE, Gregson's team chose a clean slate, starting with a 428 Police Interceptor short block. A GTA 390 hydraulic cam was stuffed inside and reworked 1963 1/2 low-riser 427 heads, featuring enlarged exhaust ports, went atop the block. A big 735-cfm Holley four-barrel carb finished things off. The result was a basically "stock" big-block Mustang, built up only with available Ford parts, that was able to turn the quarter-mile in a startling 13.39 seconds.

Ford first produced a special run of lightweight Cobra Jet Mustangs for drag racing competition. These white-painted ponies were capable of 13.5-second quarter-mile bursts right off the truck.

It was not long afterward that *Hot Rod* magazine technical editor Eric Dahlquist got wind of Tasca's work and ventured east to check out what the Bopper called his "KR-8" Mustang—"KR" for king of the road, "8" for 1968. Recognizing how easy it would be for Ford to follow in Tasca's tire tracks, Dahlquist constructed the lead page of his November 1967 *Hot Rod* coverage of the car as a ballot to help inspire the factory guys into action. Above his "Ford's Ultimate Super Cars" headline he placed two boxes marked "Yes" and "No." Below were instructions to "circle your choice in the box provided and return to: Mr. Henry Ford II, Dearborn, Michigan, 48121."

"The only way to get attention was to let Henry Ford II himself receive the responses, and boy did he get 'em," chuckled Dahlquist three decades later. "It wasn't long before a Ford public relations person was calling me asking that I 'turn off the spigot.' 'Enough already, we are going to build it.'" Though Dahlquist's efforts alone did not open the door to the Cobra Jet's creation, they certainly didn't hurt. "The next time I went back to Ford (after the *Hot Rod* article ran) I got a nice reception," he said. "The engineers were very happy."

Among those was Bill Barr, then principal design engineer in charge of the FE-series big-block V-8 program. According to him, it was Tasca who basically kicked the doors in. "Bob likes to say he was the father of the Cobra Jet, and he's right," said Barr. "When Tasca came to town, he was always immediately given an audience, and this time he flogged the company for what he wanted. He railed for the Cobra Jet, (and) that prompted us to do something like he had done."

An avid hot rodder and horsepower hound, Barr couldn't have been happier about Ford's decision late in 1967 to go ahead with the Cobra Jet. "GM products then definitely had the advantage on the street," he later recalled. "We knew the 390 Mustang would not compete with those 396 Chevelles."

Why did Dearborn officials wait so long to retaliate? "Ford was content to be a 'fast follower,'" continued Barr. "They were happy to be the producers of cars for the masses. Ford men recognized what most buyers were like. 'So many people want a car that looks like the car that went so fast.' Most didn't really want a race car-type engine." Those who did didn't have to wait long once Barr and his cohorts got rolling. "We wanted to do this thing quickly," he added, "and our advantage was that the FE had been around since the 1950s. We had a lot of parts to pick from."

Ford's FE-series V-8 dated back to 1958, appearing that year in both 332-ci and 352-ci forms. A specific high-performance version first showed two years later, the 360-horsepower 352 Interceptor Special. The FE was bored and stroked in 1961 to 390 cubic inches, and this engine was topped late that year by a dealer-installed triple-carb (a "6V" setup, in Ford parlance) option that upped output to 401 horses. Another bore job in 1962 pushed displacement to 406 cubic inches, and the 6V version of this big-block was rated at 405 horsepower. Finally, midyear in 1963, the famed 427 debuted with either a single four-barrel or dual fours. Advertised output for the former was 410 horsepower, 425 for the latter, up through 1967. Ford last offered a 427 FE in 1968, only in 390-horse single-carb form.

Nowhere near as potent as its ferocious 427 cousin, the 428 was introduced in 1966, primarily as a torque churn for turning pulleys on power steering pumps and air conditioning compressors beneath Thunderbird hoods. But being an FE, this lazy loafer still possessed an alter ego uncovered easily enough, as Tasca had proven, through a little parts interchanging.

A Cobra Jet Mustang team made big headlines at the NHRA Winternationals, held in Pomona, California, in February 1968. Al Joniec's CJ Mustang took top Super Stock honors that year, posting a 12.12-second quarter-mile pass at 109.48 miles per hour.

Barr's team began with a beefed passenger-car 428 block recast in nodular iron alloy with thickened main bearing bulkheads and extra reinforcing ribbing. Typical two-bolt main bearing caps were retained to keep costs down. Enhancing lower-end durability was left up to a nodular-iron crankshaft and burly Police Interceptor connecting rods with odd-sized 13/32-inch bolts. Pistons were cast-aluminum flat-tops. Compression was 10.6:1.

Adding those competition-conscious 427 heads was the key to Ford's Cobra Jet (CJ) transformation. Ports in these castings were predictably larger than those on their 428 counterparts, as were the valves, which measured 2.09 inches on the intake side, 1.66 on the exhaust. Additionally, the 427 heads were drilled for emissions-control plumbing and machined to accept two different exhaust manifold bolt patterns—each exhaust port face had four holes instead of two. Existing 427 FE manifolds used an over/under bolt pattern; those cast for the 1968 light-car application featured a side-by-side pattern.

Additional CJ components included a cast-iron copy of Ford's aluminum Police Interceptor intake manifold and free-flowing cast-iron exhaust manifolds. The 390 GT hydraulic cam featured 270/290 (intake/exhaust) degrees duration and 0.481/0.490 inches of lift. While the 427 and Carroll Shelby's GT-500 428 of 1967 both used dual carbs, the 428 CJ relied on a single Holley four-barrel, albeit a big one, at 735 cfm.

Advertised 428 CJ output was 335 horsepower, which didn't change with or without ram-air equipment. As Barr pointed out, dyno testing was done, of course, in a static situation with no forced induction variable injected into the equation, thus the reason for no apparent increase in the ram-air Cobra Jet's case.

The 428 CJ became the standard power source for the Fairlane Cobra, introduced in 1969. The new 429 Cobra Jet V-8 then replaced its 428 forerunner for the midsize Cobra in 1970.

Federally mandated emissions equipment also apparently didn't affect much of a change output-wise. Although many owners complained about the 428 Cobra Jet's standard Thermactor system, Barr's men "weren't overly concerned." Barr recalled, "The Thermactor didn't make that big of a difference in performance. It was not as sophisticated a design as you might think, and it did of course induce slightly more back pressure in the exhaust manifold at the exhaust valve, but I don't believe it even made as much as a 5 horsepower difference."

Ford offered the 428 Cobra Jet as a midyear 1968 1/2 option for Fairlanes, Torinos, Cougars, and midsized Mercurys, but the CJ garnered the most attention as the brave new heart of a new, truly muscular Mustang. All Cobra Jet Mustangs built in 1968 featured a functional ram-induction hood with distinctive black striping. CJ customers were also required to check off a host of extras, including, among other things, power front disc brakes and the GT equipment group, which added a heavy-duty suspension, styled steel wheels wearing F70 rubber, C-stripes, fog lamps, and chrome exhaust tips.

As for the name, no one is really sure who deserves credit, although it's obvious where the Cobra theme originated. According to Bob Tasca, Lee Iacocca had paid a high price for the rights to Shelby's sneaky snake label and wasn't about to see all that cash go to waste. From there, it was more or less a matter of evolution.

"We already had the snake idea in our heads," Barr explained. "And we didn't do this like we normally did. We didn't just roll out the product with everyone standing around it, scratching their asses trying to name it. The idea was already rolling by that stage. Some artist in Styling had already created a drawing of the Cobra emblem—the snake with the wheels and exhausts coming out of its tale. We had the drawing; then the name came from there." Some over the years have inferred that the Cobra Jet moniker was perhaps a knock-off of Chevy's existing "Turbo-Jet" V-8 references, but Barr disagreed. "The sales guys didn't necessarily try to one-up Chevrolet. They just might have misinterpreted that drawing, thinking those exhausts in back were jets."

Witnesses who first experienced Cobra Jet performance probably saw things similarly. "We'd been testing a lot of cars," said Eric Dahlquist, "and Fords had been way at the back of the pack. Then this Mustang shows up, and it's a rocket ship. Ford from last to first in one jump." Barr added, "Once you went down on the loud pedal, this baby could really fly. On the street, the Cobra Jet was absolutely awesome. Nothing I saw anywhere could touch it. For stoplight Grand Prixs, the 428 Cobra Jet was the bee's knees, because nothing could stay with it."

Barr's engineering tests of a box-stock Cobra Jet Mustang pilot car put quarter-mile performance at 13.4 seconds. According to him, all CJ Mustangs sold in 1968 were potentially that quick. "When we saw the magazine test scores of about a 13.6, we figured they must have had a poor driver." The results Barr referred to were published in *Hot Rod*'s March 1968 by Dahlquist, who had pressed Dearborn for a first look at a Cobra Jet in exchange for "turning off the spigot." After watching a still-sizzling 13.56-second run, he concluded that "the CJ will be the utter delight of every Ford lover and the bane of all the rest because, quite frankly, it is probably the fastest regular-production sedan ever built."

Ford's 428 Cobra Jet returned for 1969, this time as standard equipment beneath the hood of the new Fairlane Cobra. It was optional on all other Fairlanes, as well as the Mustang. In the latter's case, the GT package was no longer a mandatory feature, nor was the ram-air equipment automatically included the previous year. The basic 1969 428 CJ came topped with a conventional single-snorkel air cleaner fitted with a vacuum-operated pop-off valve that sprung open at full throttle to improve airflow. Once again, that 335-horse rating stayed the same, with ram air or without.

The one thing that did increase in 1969 was the ram-air CJ's image. Beneath the '68 1/2 CJ Mustang's hood was an air cleaner that sealed to the hood's underside to allow cooler, denser outside air an easier passage from the functional scoop above into that Holley's four throats. In 1969, that conventional scoop was traded for the legendary "Shaker," which attached directly to the top of the air cleaner and protruded up through an opening in the hood. When the Cobra Jet started shaking side to side under torque load, so too did this ribbed, black scoop—thus the formal name.

Inside the sinister black Shaker was a vacuum-controlled bypass flap that automatically opened wide whenever the pedal met the metal, allowing outside air to ram into the four waiting venturi with far less restriction. Normally, the ram-air 428 CJ sucked in heated underhood atmosphere through the air cleaner's conventional snorkel.

As for that never-changing output rating, those in the know knew better. When *Car and Driver*'s lead-footers tested a '69 428 Cobra Jet Mach 1, they taped the Shaker's opening shut and instantly recorded an 0.2-second and 2-mile-per-hour decrease in quarter-mile performance. "Ford can be justifiably proud," read *Car and Driver*'s conclusions concerning the Shaker. "It works."

Ford engineers were also proud of another optional addition to the CJ performance package. A 428 Cobra Jet became a Super Cobra Jet whenever a buyer checked off the "Drag Pack" rear-axle option, which consisted of either a 3.91:1 or 4.30:1 strip-ready axle ratio in a Traction-Lok limited-slip differential. Recognizing that these gears were best suited for on-track action, the engineering team further built up the CJ into the SCJ by adding tougher forged-aluminum pistons (in place of the CJ's cast slugs) and beefy "LeMans" rods. Developed for Ford's GT-40 427, these superstrong connecting rods were held onto the crank by cap screws and larger 7/16-inch rod bolts instead of conventional nuts and the Cobra Jet's standard 13/32-inch bolts. Adding these heavier rods and pistons of course required rebalancing the engine, so an external counter-balancer (among other things) was incorporated behind the crank's vibration damper. A racing-style external oil cooler was mounted on the front of the radiator core support on the driver's side to complete the Super Cobra Jet package.

The 428 Cobra Jet remained a strong street performance option through 1970 but only for Ford Motor Company's pony cars, the Mustang and its Cougar cousin. Production of 428 Cobra Jet and Super Cobra Mustangs for 1969 and 1970 was 13,193 and 2,671, respectively, bringing the total three-year run to 18,691 before Ford finally ended the long-in-the-tooth FE-series big-block run.

Ford's new 385-series 429 Cobra Jet replaced its 428 FE forerunner in other 1970 models, including the hot Torino Cobra. Even though he also contributed to the second-edition CJ, Bill Barr wasn't necessarily convinced that progress in this case was a good thing. According to him, "a 429 Cobra Jet never beat a 428 Cobra Jet" in in-house tests. No way, no how.

Above, right: A ram-air hood was included with the 428 Cobra Jet in Mustang applications in 1968; it became an option the following year. But with or without the sporty Shaker, the CJ V-8 remained rated at 335 horsepower.

Right: This oil cooler was one of various modifications made in 1969 to transform a Cobra Jet into a Super Cobra Jet.

Initially only offered in midsize B-body ranks in 1969, Dodge's 440 Six-Pack V-8 also became an option for the new E-body 'Cuda in 1970. Like its Hemi sibling, the Six-Pack 'Cuda was treated to the high-profile Shaker hood scoop.

CHAPTER 19

Triple Threat: Dodge's 440 Six-Pack V-8

It's not easy to get lost in a brother's shadow when you're notably larger than said sibling, but that's just what happened to Chrysler Corporation's 440-cubic-inch big-block V-8 back in the 1960s.

Type: water-cooled OHV 90-degree RB-series V-8

Construction: cast-iron block and cylinder heads

Main bearings: five

Bore and stroke: 4.32x3.75 inches

Displacement: 440 cubic inches

Valves: two per cylinder (2.08-inch intakes, 1.74-inch exhausts), with heavy-duty Hemi valve springs

Camshaft: hydraulic lifters

Compression: 10.5:1

Induction: three Holley two-barrel carburetors

Horsepower: 390 at 5,200 rpm

Torque: 490 at 3,200 rpm

Adding triple carburetors to the 440 big block upped the output ante from 375 horsepower to 390.

Though it was later superseded by General Motors' 454- and 455-cube big-blocks in 1970, Dodge and Plymouth's 440 V-8 briefly stood as Detroit's heftiest muscle car motor after joining the high-performance ranks in 1967. Yet early on, it still commonly ranked low in the minds of many outside of the Chrysler realm, thanks to the dominating presence of its smaller brethren, the 426 street Hemi. Of course, honestly speaking, the Hemi did deserve the lion's share of the limelight, being so much more powerful and significantly successful in competition circles. That mighty Mopar had it all: 425 token-rated horses, superbad looks, a street rep as the meanest muscle car mill to ever roast a wide tread. And let's not forget its high price.

Ah, the rub. Like its Firepower forerunner from the 1950s, the 426 Hemi was far and away Chrysler's costliest engine to build, and the 426 option was every bit as hard on customers' wallets. An extra grand or so was a real wad in 1966, certainly so for an engine alone. Hell, at about $2,700, the car the Hemi was going into that year represented a bargain in comparison. So too did the 440, which brings us to the reason for this big bully's being, as well as that of the engine family it sprang from.

The 440's roots run back to 1958, when Chrysler officials decided to save fuss, muss, and money by switching back to conventional wedge-head engines. The big 392-ci Firepower V-8 was retired that year, ending a powerful legacy dating back to 1951. DeSoto and Dodge had dropped their smaller hemi-head V-8s the previous year, replacing them with Chrysler's new, lighter, far less complex B-series big-block V-8, with its typical inline valve layout, that now required only one rocker shaft instead of the two needed for the hemi head's inclined valves. All B engines from then up through the bloodline's demise in 1978 relied on the same stroke—3.375 inches—and matching that crank with a 4.06-inch bore resulted in the 350-ci wedge-head V-8 that both DeSoto and Plymouth unveiled for 1958. Increasing the B-series block's bore to 4.125 inches produced the 361 wedge, which DeSoto also used that year along with Dodge.

Chrysler Division, meanwhile, turned to an even larger B-series variant for 1959 to replace the vaunted 392 Hemi in its upscale ranks. Known as an "RB," or "tall-deck," V-8, this new powerplant was simply a B engine with a raised (thus the "R") cylinder block deck, a casting modification made to increase displacement potential by allowing for a longer stroke. Deck surface to crank centerline within a "low-deck" B engine measured 9.980 inches; the distance in the RB block was 10.725 inches. This extra deck height in turn made room for a 3.750-inch stroke, which remained constant during the RB's run up through 1978. In 1959, this stroke was paired with a 4.180-inch bore to create 413 cubic inches. Another RB, the little-known 383 V-8, also appeared briefly for 1959 and 1960 (with a 4.03-inch bore) and shouldn't be confused with the much more popular low-deck 383 V-8 that debuted in 1961. The bore in the B-series 383 was 4.250 inches.

Though primarily a quiet giant meant mostly for luxury liner applications, the 413 V-8 did work well as the heart of Chrysler's letter-car line from 1959 to 1965, maxing out at 405 horsepower as an option for the 300H in 1962. That same year, both Dodge and Plymouth began offering the meanest, nastiest 413 ever, the so-called "Max Wedge," with its cross-ram dual-carb intake and high-flying headerlike exhaust manifolds. Clearly meant only for the drag strip, the 413 Max Wedge came in two forms depending on compression levels: 410 horsepower with an 11:1 squeeze or 420 with a molecule-mashing 13.5:1 ratio.

An even larger 426 Max Wedge appeared in 1963 after RB bore was increased yet again to 4.250 inches. Known as the "Stage II" wedge, this tall-block V-8 was rated at 415 and 425

The triple-carb 440 V-8 debuted in 1969 as part of a race-ready package offered by both Dodge and Plymouth. Like its 440 Six-Barrel Road Runner running mate from Plymouth, Dodge's 1969 Six-Pack Super Bee was delivered sans wheel covers and hood hinges. The latter simply lifted off by hand.

horsepower. An improved Stage III V-8 also appeared that year; then the Max Wedge was replaced early in 1964 by the outrageous 426-ci race Hemi.

A civilized version of the 426 wedge debuted as well, late in 1964, though few seemingly noticed the RB big-block described by Plymouth advertisements as a "street version of our competition-designed 426 Hemi engine, which holds more records than our competitors care to count." In truth, save for displacement, this 365-horsepower 426 had little in common with the vaunted race Hemi. Both Dodge and Plymouth offered this relatively strong, rarely seen, performance option into 1965.

Then along came the 426 street Hemi to change all the rules. Yes, this legendary motor instantly became king of the streets. But, as mentioned, it wasn't cheap, and thus wasn't produced in great numbers. At the time, both Plymouth's GTX and Dodge's Coronet R/T were waiting in the wings for 1967, and each was counted on to find far more buyers than the high-priced Hemi initially did in 1966. Hemi power was optional for both, but new standard muscle was needed if costs were to be kept down and excitement up. That new mill was the 440.

Created in 1966 by increasing the RB block's bore to a hefty 4.320 inches, Chrysler's "440 TNT" big-block was at first little more than a beastly torque churn best suited to propel luxury liners along. TNT output that year was 350 horsepower, but potential for much more oomph was clearly present. To this end came better-breathing open-chamber heads, freer-flowing exhaust manifolds, a big Carter four-barrel carb, and a more aggressive hydraulic cam in 1967 to help boost output to 375 horsepower for what Dodge called its 440 Magnum V-8. Plymouth's counterpart was the 440 Super Commando.

While compression (10.1:1) was the same for the TNT and its 375-horse alter ego, that latter RB V-8 was topped off with a low-restriction, dual-snorkel air cleaner to help its Carter carb suck like nobody's business. Modifications also included a revised valvetrain better suited to handle the lumpier cam's reciprocating demands. High-load valve springs helped resist valve float, and those springs incorporated surge dampers to limit unwanted harmonics. At 2.08 inches, intake valve size carried over from the TNT, but exhaust diameter was enlarged from 1.60 inches to 1.74 for the Magnum/Super Commando. The Magnum was the '67 Coronet R/T's standard power source; the Super Commando was the GTX's.

While some R/T and GTX customers did choose the optional Hemi, the majority stuck with the 375-horse 440, losing little in the deal, face or otherwise. What the 440 lacked in horsepower, it made up for in overall ease of use compared to its cantankerous solid-lifter

Three Holley two-barrel carburetors gave the Six-Pack its name.

Chrysler engineers were especially creative during the 1960s and 1970s when it came to speeding spent gases on their way.

cousin. As *Hot Rod* magazine's Dick Scritchfield explained, the heart-and-soul of the 1967 GTX was "a street engine with racing ability without the problems of the finely tuned racing mill."

The 440 initially wasn't offered as an option for Plymouth's Road Runner and Dodge's Super Bee when they debuted for 1968. But that changed in 1969. New that summer were two special models, the 440 Six-Pack Super Bee and its 440 Six-Barrel Road Runner running mate, both outfitted identically to go right from the dealer's lot to the drag strip. Included in each deal was a new 390-horsepower 440 created most notably by substituting the 375-horsepower big block's single Carter carburetor for three Holley two-barrels mounted on an aluminum Edelbrock intake manifold. Flow for the 375-horsepower 440's one Carter was 650 cfm. Those three Holleys equaled 990 cfm, with the center one flowing 250, the two ends 370. Externally, the only other addition was a dual-point distributor.

Triple-carb induction arrangements had been tried on various occasions by various automakers prior to 1969. Earliest out of Detroit was the setup seen in 1953 on the first Corvette's Blue Flame six-cylinder, followed four years later by Oldsmobile's J2 package and Pontiac's well-known Tri Power. Cadillac, Lincoln, and Mercury all tried triple carburetors to help haul some seriously large bodies around in 1958, and Chevrolet that year introduced a three-deuce option for its new 348-ci V-8, as did Ford for its FE-series big block in 1961. Olds and Pontiac were still offering tricarb induction as late as 1966, after which time GM officials banned multiple-carburetor options on all the divisions' cars, save for the Corvette. That said, the Corvette then emerged in 1967 with a "3x2" 427 V-8 that made 435 rompin', stompin' horses.

Like the Corvette's setup, the three two-barrels on the Mopar 440 relied on vacuum, as opposed to mechanical, linkage to decide when all three throats would sing together. Internally, the triple-carb and four-barrel 440 V-8s were essentially the same as far as compression and cam timing were concerned, but the 390-horsepower version was equipped for higher revolutions, thanks to various items taken off the high-performance parts shelf. Stiff Hemi valve springs, beefed-up rocker arms and connecting rods, molybdenum-filled piston rings, and flash-chromed valves were used, while cam lobes and lifter surfaces were specially machined to equalize wear typically realized when high-tension valve springs were slamming the valves back shut. Mopar engineers had discovered earlier the damage Hemi valve springs could do to an unsuspecting cam; in some cases, owners were flattening lobes after only 10,000 miles. As the cam lobes actuated the lifters inside the 390-horsepower 440 engine, the lifters would rotate, distributing wear more evenly over friction surfaces.

Other heavy-duty components were packaged with the triple-carb 440, including a maximum-capacity cooling system, the fully beefed Hemi suspension, 4.10:1 Sure-Grip gears in a 9.75 Dana 60 rear end, and G70x15 Goodyear Polyglas tires mounted on 15x6 wheels. No wheel covers were included: those black-painted wheels were simply adorned with chrome lug nuts, nothing else.

Hood hinges also were left off both the Six-Barrel Road Runner and Six-Pack Super Bee. Standard was a fiberglass lid that simply lifted off by hand (two pairs, that is) once four chrome-plated locking pins were released. "All very racy, but we're sure the novelty of the two-man hood would wear off quickly," observed *Car Life*'s critics. That lift-off hood also incorporated a large, wide-open scoop that directed cooler outside air into a waiting air cleaner below that was sealed to the hood's underside by a large rubber doughnut. Again in *Car Life*'s words, that scoop "gapes wide open, seemingly ready to ingest all that gets near it, including water, dirt, or birds." Special drain tubes in the air cleaner took care of the water; birds were on their own.

Priced considerably less than their Hemi-powered counterparts, the Six-Barrel Road Runner and Six-Pack Super Bee were every bit as quick, if not quicker than their vaunted running mates. In a *Super Stock* magazine road test, a 390-horsepower 440 Road Runner averaged 13.50 seconds and 109.31 miles per hour for the quarter-mile. Being a bigger bang for the buck surely was a fair claim. As *Hot Rod*'s Steve Kelly explained, "If the price and temperament of a hemi-head engine haven't been enough to thoroughly discourage street-driving performance-car buyers from ordering the 426 in their new Dodge (or Plymouth), then the new 390-horsepower Mopar Six-Pack option will deal the final blow."

Even fewer bucks were required in 1970, as the triple-carb 440 V-8 returned as an engine option alone without the extra mandatory features. The strip-ready '69 Six-Pack Super Bee and Six-Barrel Road Runner ended up being one-hit wonders. Midsized customers who chose the 390-horse 440 in 1970 also received hood hinges and wheel covers, or perhaps those attractive new Rallye wheels. Other changes included the substitution of a less-expensive cast-iron intake in place of the previously used aluminum unit and the insertion of beefier connecting rods with noticeable wider beam sections. Adding these heavier rods in turn created a need for external balancing, a first for a Chrysler engine.

The 390-horse 440 V-8 became an option for Chrysler's two new E-bodies in 1970—Dodge's Challenger and Plymouth's 'Cuda—and either of these models could've been fitted as well with another new option, the huge Shaker scoop that poked right through an opening in the hood to breathe directly from the cooler atmosphere outside the engine compartment. E-bodies and their bigger B-body midsized models were once more offered with the Six-Pack/Six-Barrel option in 1971 before the axe finally fell on Detroit's ferocious factory hot rods.

Like the 426 Hemi, the triple-carb 440 faded from the scene at year's end, leaving only some serious tire smoke behind.

Like the 426 Hemi, the triple-carb 440 was last seen in 1971. Production that year of Plymouth's 440+6 GTX hardtop (shown here) was a mere 135.

At 450 horsepower, Chevrolet's 454-cubic-inch LS6 V-8 was the highest-rated engine produced during Detroit's original muscle car era. The LS6 was an SS454 Chevelle option for 1970 only. A 425-horse LS6 followed for the 1971 Corvette.

CHAPTER 20

Maximum Muscle: Chevrolet LS6 454 V-8

Factory hot rods were seemingly everywhere you looked in 1970, with

even staid, stoic Wisconsin-based American

Motors caught up in the fury by then. Hemi

Mopars, Cobra Jet Fords, Stage 1 Buicks—the

list went on and on and on. But there still was

only one king of the high-performance hill

that year.

Type: water-cooled OHV 90-degree Mk.IV big-block V-8

Construction: cast-iron block and cylinder heads, inclined valves

Main bearings: five

Bore and stroke: 4.25x4.00 inches

Displacement: 454 cubic inches

Valves: two per cylinder (2.19-inch intakes, 1.88-inch exhausts)

Camshaft: solid lifters (0.520-inch lift)

Compression: 11.25:1 (TRW forged-aluminum pistons)

Induction: 780-cfm Holley four-barrel carburetor

Horsepower: 450 at 5,200 rpm

Torque: 500 at 3,600 rpm

Chevrolet's first modern big block, called the Mk. II, appeared in 1963 in race-only form. Called the "Mystery Motor" by the press, this 427-cubic-inch mill wowed witnesses at Daytona that year, producing speeds in excess of 165 miles per hour. Key to the Mystery Motor's success was its cylinder head design, which featured free-breathing canted valves.

Pontiac's GTO, the car that had kicked off Detroit's supercar craze in 1964, had lost its crown (from a purely popular standpoint) in 1969 to the muscle-bound midsized Chevrolet first seen in 1965: the big-block Super Sport Chevelle. From 1964 to 1968, the GTO had reigned as America's best-selling muscle car. From 1969 on, however, it was the Chevelle SS that led the way on the hit parade.

The heart of this ground-pounding beast was Chevrolet's Mk. IV V-8, introduced early in 1965 as an option for the Chevelle SS, Caprice, and Corvette. Mk. IV roots ran back to July 1962, when engineer Dick Keinath created a modernized big-block V-8 to supersede the fabled 409 in competition circles. Called the Mk. II, this 427-cubic-inch racing mill represented a marked departure from the rather archaic W-head, resembling its cousin only slightly on the bottom end. From there all bets were off.

On top of the Mk. II was a pair of superb cylinder heads that breathed better than perhaps anything ever seen before out of Detroit. Soon known as "porcupine" heads, these castings featured canted valves that protruded up from the combustion chambers at varying angles, looking very much like the haphazard quills on the back of a pesky ... well, you know. This innovative arrangement was made possible by Chevrolet's proven ball-stud rocker arm design, an idea that had helped make the Hot One so hot in 1955. Not only did ball-stud rockers greatly reduce valvetrain weight, they also allowed engineers to place the valves where they would work best. And instead of designing the all-important combustion chamber around a limited, conventional inline valve position, the ball-stud rockers' flexibility gave those engineers the newfound freedom to shape the chambers almost any way they liked.

The porcupine heads' intake valves were located up high near their ports and inclined slightly, making for a straighter flow from intake manifold to combustion chamber. An opposite inclination was applied (to a slightly lesser degree) on the exhaust end to the same effect. In between, those valves opened into a modified wedge combustion chamber that some classified as a "semi-hemi." Like Chrysler's legendary hemispherical chamber design, Chevy's modified wedge featured improved flame propagation and excellent volumetric efficiency. And the inclined valve setup also allowed for a bit more room in those chambers for truly big valves, just the ticket to let more of the good air/fuel in and get the bad out.

These wonderfully efficient heads helped the Mk. II 427 make a whopping 520 horsepower on the dyno, and all this muscle of course translated into comparable big numbers at the track. Labeled the "Mystery Motor" by the press, Chevrolet's new big-block wowed the crowd at Daytona in February 1963 with speeds in excess of 165 miles per hour. A Mystery Motor Chevy won both 100-mile Daytona 500 qualifiers that year, but mechanical failures allowed Fords to dominate the big show. Disappointing, sure, but the Mk. II already was history even before the checkered flag dropped on the Daytona 500. General Motor's infamous antiracing edict, sent down a month before, had decided that. But fortunately the story didn't end there.

Although initial reports claimed an abrupt end of the line for Chevrolet's latest, greatest big block, former Hudson man Vince Piggins—by then hawking horsepower at GM's entry-level division—just wouldn't have it. In April 1963, he proposed installing the Mystery Motor in the all-new A-body Chevelle, then awaiting its debut as a 1964 model. His plan involved using a 396-cubic-inch derivative, achieved by reducing the stillborn 427 V-8's bore from 4.25 inches to 4.09 (stroke for both was 3.76 inches). But various glitches delayed development of this package for another year. As it was, GM had already put a 330-ci limit on its midsized models, making Piggins' proposed combination taboo.

Three different air cleaners were used atop the LS6 in 1970: a typical open-element unit, a rare dual-snorkel housing, and the familiar cowl induction equipment, removed in this case.

But Pontiac people simply ignored that limit in 1964 when they introduced their GTO with 389 standard cubes. GM officials, with perhaps just a bit of egg on their faces, then responded by raising the lid to 400 cubic inches for 1965, just in time for Chevrolet to roll out its aptly named SS 396 Chevelle in February. Beneath the first SS 396's hood was the new Turbo-Jet Mk. IV big block, a hydraulic-lifter V-8 rated at 375 horsepower for the A-body application. Another 396, this one using solid tappets, produced 425 brutal horses for the '65 Corvette, while a third (also with hydraulic lifters) was rated at 325 horsepower for the Caprice.

The Mystery Motors' original bore size was then restored for the Corvette's optional Mk. IV big block in 1966, though advertised output for this new 427 Mk. IV remained at 425 horsepower. It reached a maximum of 435 horses in 1967, when three two-barrel carburetors were added atop the Corvette's meanest optional big block, though that wasn't necessarily the limit for the 427 that year. RPO L88, a rare race-only option that added aluminum heads to a radically modified 427, reportedly produced 430 horsepower, but that was clearly a token rating. Actual output easily exceeded 550 horses.

LS6 heads in 1970 were closed-chamber units cast in iron. The makeup changed to aluminum for the 1971 LS6 Corvette.

Staying within its limits, the SS 396 Chevelle—as its name implied—continued on with the 396-ci Mk. IV, but that certainly wasn't a bad thing. Top optional output from 1966 to 1969 was 375 horsepower, more than enough oomph to help make the SS 396 America's most popular muscle car. By 1970, the SS 396 legacy was so deeply entrenched that Chevrolet promotional people didn't dare toy with the name after the A-body Turbo-Jet big block was bored out to 402 cubic inches. "Ess-ess-four-oh-two?" No way. It was "ess-ess-three-ninety-six" or nothing at all—unless, of course, "it" was the new SS 454, the supreme evolvement of the breed.

The SS 454 Chevelle came into being after GM's party poopers finally dropped that 400-cube displacement limit for 1970, opening the door for additional escalation in the midsized performance field. Both Oldsmobile and Buick introduced 455-ci big-block V-8s for the 4-4-2 and Gran Sport, respectively, while Chevrolet engineers stroked their Mk. IV V-8 (from 3.76 inches to 4.00) to end up with 454 cubes. A 390-horse version (RPO LS5) of this bigger big block replaced the 427 on the 1970 Corvette's options list.

Not all engineers at Chevrolet, however, thought that more cubes represented the key to bigger and better things. Development man Tom Langdon, who had worked on Chevrolet's exotic all-aluminum ZL-1 427 V-8 in 1969, never was a big fan of the biggest Mk. IV. "Increasing the stroke without enlarging the bore doesn't necessarily translate into a real increase in power," he said in 1999. "Some of that extra power is eaten up by increased friction. A good (L88) 427 would put out about 600 horsepower. The 454 pulled more torque (on the dyno), but power was just about the same as the L88."

Langdon also wasn't sure about the 454's stamina under stress. "The L88 already had demonstrated substantial durability problems," he continued. "A longer stroke inherently creates more problems through increased friction. Increasing the stroke, to go from 427 cubic inches to 454, only aggravated the (Mk. IV's) problems. We hadn't even solved the 427's problems yet, and we were making (them) worse."

Maybe so, but that didn't stop Chevrolet from making the jump up the displacement ladder. Zora Duntov's people even planned to continue the L88 legacy into 1970, announcing the 454-ci aluminum-head LS7 as a Corvette option that year. Mystery and confusion surrounded this big-block beast right from the start, beginning with 1970 Corvette brochures that listed it at 465 horsepower, compared to early assembly manuals that pegged it at 460. No matter, though; the LS7 was canceled as part of a performance de-escalation, leaving the much more civilized LS5 454 as the fiberglass two-seater's hottest option (and only available big block) that year.

Two 454 Mk. IV big blocks were offered for the 1970 Chevelle, beginning with the A-body line's own LS5, rated at a relatively tame 360 horsepower. The other was the legendary LS6, a certifiably potent powerplant that *Car Life* called "the best supercar engine ever released by General Motors." Many other critics considered the LS6 to be the best supercar engine, period.

Put together with care at Chevrolet's big-block V-8 production plant in Tonawanda, New York, the LS6 454 was specially built from oil pan to air cleaner with truly super performance in mind. Unlike the LS5, which was based on a two-bolt main bearing block, the LS6's bottom end was held together with four-bolt main bearing caps. And the block itself featured pretapped holes for a race-ready external oiling system.

The LS6 crank was a tuftrided, forged 5140 alloy steel piece that was cross-drilled to ensure ample oil supply to the connecting rod bearings. Rods were forged steel, magnafluxed for rigidity, with 7/16-inch bolts, compared to the LS5's 3/8-inch units. At the rods' business ends were TRW forged aluminum pistons, which mashed the mixture at a ratio of 11.25:1. LS5 compression was 10.25:1. A definitely aggressive cam (0.520-inch lift, 316-degree duration) activated solid lifters, while beefy 3/8-inch pushrods and heavy-duty dual valve springs completed the valvetrain.

Perhaps the main attraction involved the LS6's cast-iron, closed-chamber cylinder heads, which could breathe like blue blazes thanks to large rectangular ports and big valves: 2.19-inch intakes, 1.88-inch exhausts. A huge 780-cfm Holley four-barrel fed this brute, which was conservatively rated by Chevrolet at 450 horsepower, the highest advertised output figure ever assigned to a muscle car engine. Some claim actual output was more than 500 horses. Whatever the number, the results on the street were outrageous.

"Driving a 450-horsepower Chevelle is like being the guy who's in charge of triggering atom bomb tests," claimed a *Super Stock* report. "You have the power, you know you have the power, and you know if you use the power, bad things may happen. Things like arrest, prosecution, loss of license, broken pieces, shredded tires, etc."

Even so, Grandpa Elmer's wife probably could've driven this car down the quarter-mile in a click more than 13 seconds. Dipping into the 12s was only a matter of letting Grandma slap on a pair of slicks and bolt on a set of headers while her cookies cooled on the ledge. Either way, the LS6 Chevelle was all but unbeatable on the street. "That's 'LS' as in land-speed record," concluded *Motor Trend*'s A. B. Shuman.

That kind of performance from a car Granny might also have been almost willing to drive to the store helped rank the LS6 Chevelle right at the top of the muscle car heap. The car not

LS5 454 cylinder blocks featured two-bolt main bearing caps. LS6 lower ends were held together by four-bolt mains.

A larger 780-cfm Holley four-barrel carburetor crowned the LS6 454 V-8.

only was a mean machine, it could also get along relatively well with everyday use. Evidence of just how well appeared perhaps in production figures. Even though the 450-horse 454 alone cost $1,000 extra, the slightly cranky LS6 Chevelle actually outsold its more affordable, less disagreeable LS5 brother, 4,475 to 4,298. While rivals like the W-30 455 Olds, 455 Stage 1 GSX from Buick, Pontiac's Ram Air IV Trans Am, and Ford's 429 CJ Torino Cobra could keep pace with the LS6 when the light turned green, not one could match its market saturation. Detroit's most powerful muscle car was also its greatest (relatively speaking) sales success.

A second-edition LS6 Chevelle was initially planned for 1971, and at least one pilot model was delivered to the press late in 1970 for road testing. But, like the '70 LS7 Corvette, this midsized monster was killed off before it could do Tokyo even the slightest harm. At least the LS6 Mk. IV survived, this time as an option for the 1971 Corvette.

Different sources have different explanations for the fact that the Corvette didn't get its own LS6 option in 1970, leaving it in the uncustomary position of playing second fiddle in Chevrolet's power-producing pecking order. Some, including Tom Langdon, have since claimed that the 450-horsepower 454 didn't carry up into Corvette ranks earlier than it did due to the lack of a suitable low-rise intake manifold able to fit beneath the two-seater's low, low hood.

Perhaps more crucial to the issue was Chevrolet's 1970 last-minute lineup evolutions. Even though early paperwork also had the Chevelle getting its own LS7 454 that year, the proposed 465-horsepower Corvette still would've claimed no less than a tie for Chevrolet's top power spot in 1970. Planners apparently never even considered an LS6 option for the '70 Corvette, with the LS7 deal all but inked. Mention of an LS7 Chevelle option then quickly evaporated, leaving the promised LS7 Corvette to roll on toward Chevrolet's late-starting 1970 production run with intentions of once again standing alone atop the division's performance pyramid. According to engineer Gib Hufstader, once the LS7 was canceled it was too late to call up the LS6 as a stand-in.

Why the LS6 then appeared on the Corvette's option list but not the Chevelle's for 1971 probably involved the plain fact that most in Detroit recognized that the end of the road was in sight for the great American muscle car. Compression cuts across the board for nearly all automakers' engines awaited buyers that year, which was the last for such internal combustion legends as Chrysler's Hemi and Ford's 429 Cobra Jet. Though the SS 454 Chevelle did return for 1971, it relied only on the mild LS5 Mk. IV big block. The days of 450-horsepower midsized muscle cars clearly were over.

The Corvette, on the other hand, existed only to excite, and thus was treated to one last big burst of horsepower in 1971, before things started cooling off around Detroit. That year's LS6 V-8 wasn't spared from the compression-cutting axe, however, and lost some ponies as the air/fuel crush was dropped to 9:1. Advertised output was 425 horsepower that time around.

On the positive side were the aluminum, open-chamber cylinder heads bolted on in place of the iron units used in 1970. Much of the rest of the 1971 LS6's makeup again mimicked the L88, save for those low-compression pistons (which remained TRW forged aluminum pieces) with their decreased dome heights. On top, a 780-cfm Holley four-barrel sat on a low-rise, dual-plane intake cast of aluminum. The solid-lifter cam bumped up both valves by 0.519 inch through 1.7:1 stamped steel rockers. Duration was 316 degrees on the intake side, 302 on the exhaust. Ignition was transistorized.

The price for RPO LS6 in 1971 was $1,220, leaving little wonder why only 188 customers checked off the aluminum-head 454 option that year, a disappointing result that Zora Duntov took full blame for. "Maybe for street engine I make mistake," he admitted in his familiar broken English to *Car and Driver*. "Aluminum heads are expensive and that weight (loss) doesn't matter on the street."

Even more expensive, and much rarer, was RPO ZR-2, which included the LS6 V-8 within a package that, among other things, also added a kidney-rattling, race-ready suspension. Price for the ZR-2 option was $1,747. Only 12 were built, all hopefully going to serious racers only. Like the L88 Corvettes of 1967–1969, the gnarly '71 ZR-2 was never meant for the street, and those who foolishly tried taking one there quickly found out why. Driving without a radio (deleted as part of this competition-conscious deal) was only the least of the troubles involved.

Neither the uncivilized ZR-2 nor the LS6 454 returned for 1972, the first of many ever-darkening years for anguished American horsepower hounds. Chevrolet's 454-ci LS5 did survive through two more years, but it just wasn't the same. And by 1975, as far as Corvette buyers were concerned, it was small block or no block.

LS6 Chevelles outnumbered their less-impressive LS5 counterparts in 1970, 4,475 to 4,298. Both LS6 coupes and convertibles were built that year.

Ford's turbocharged SVO four-cylinder produced 175 horsepower from only 140 cubic inches—a truly amazing feat for the time.

CHAPTER 21

Mighty Mite: Ford SVO Mustang Turbo Four-Cylinder

What goes up generally must come down, and such was the case for the

great American V-8. After supplanting the old, reliable six-cylinder

as Detroit's bread-and-butter power source during the 1950s, the modern

V-8 rapidly grew in both size and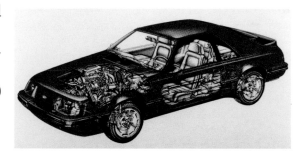

strength. By 1970, Chevrolet's 454-

cubic-inch big block was making 450

horsepower in maxed-out form.

Ford announced the formation of its Special Vehicle Operations in September 1980, with the goal to create "a series of limited-production performance cars and develop their image through motorsport." Ford of Europe competition director Michael Kranefuss was brought across the Atlantic to run SVO.

But then along came tightening emissions standards and soaring fuel prices. Almost overnight, Detroit's beastliest V-8s were transformed into dinosaurs, and the breed itself was, in some minds, nearing extinction as the 1980s dawned. That didn't happen, of course, but into the void created by the V-8's fade came an engine that long, long ago used to rule the roost in America: the inline four-cylinder.

Though Yankees weren't strangers to four-cylinder engines during the 1960s (General Motors offered a couple), the two groups grew really close in the early 1970s, thanks to a newfound need to skimp on fuel. Europeans, on the other hand, never had lost touch with the four-banger due to an undying demand overseas for supereconomical, supersmall cars. So it was, then, that when the latest compact craze hit America 35 years ago, it was driven primarily by foreign-sourced powerplants. Such was the case at Ford, which rolled out its new Pinto for 1971 with a British-built 1.6-liter four as standard equipment and a German-built 2.0-liter four as an option. Both engines were of overhead-cam design.

While Ford obviously didn't introduce a modern four-cylinder to the U.S. market, it was this country's metric pioneer. Dearborn's first domestic-built four—the 2.3-liter OHC engine created for the downsized, Pinto-based Mustang II—also was the first all-metric engine manufactured in America, this due to engineers' desires to preserve parts interchangeability with the company's Euro-sourced four-cylinders. Introduced for 1974, Ford's in-house four produced 85 horsepower. And for those of you who still have an aversion to metric wrenches, those 2.3 liters translated into 140 cubic inches.

Reactions to Ford's four-cylinder revival were mixed. Being one of those "right cars for the times," the Pinto initially did well, as did its cousin, the Mustang II, during its first year out of the corral. But loyal Mustang buyers expected more out of their pride and joys, and complaints of truly cramped quarters quickly drowned out 1974's raves, which included *Motor Trend*'s "Car of the Year" honors. An optional V-6 (Euro-sourced as well) also left customers flat, leading to a 51 percent sales slide for 1975. Ford's 302-cubic-inch Windsor V-8 appeared as a new option that year, but it wasn't strong enough to save the day, and the disappointing Mustang II was history within three years.

That the Mustang lost much of its fun face during the 1970s was no coincidence, as Henry Ford II by then had become a real party pooper. A staunch racing supporter during the 1960s, he didn't blink an eye late in 1970 when he axed his company's once-proud motorsports program to concentrate on more socially responsible projects, like operating cleaner-running factories that built fuel-efficient cars. Performance truly became a dirty word around Dearborn and remained so throughout most of the decade.

But the 1980s brought new leadership, and under President Donald Petersen's direction, Ford engineers found it fun to build cars again. Their Fox-chassis Mustang, which had replaced Lee Iacocca's Mustang II in 1979, represented the first turn toward more kicks. Next was a new organization dedicated to putting the Blue Oval back in action at the track.

Announced in September 1980, Ford's Special Vehicle Operations department was formed to create "a series of limited-production performance cars and develop their image through motorsport." Michael Kranefuss, who had previously been competition director for Ford of Europe, was brought across the Atlantic to run SVO, and he wasted little time putting the latest-generation pony car to work on IMSA and SCCA road-racing courses. As for a limited-production performance car for the street, that long-rumored model finally came along about four years later.

A major blast of fresh air, the 1984 SVO Mustang wowed press critics with its sensational performance, supplied, by of all the things, Ford's 2.3-liter four-cylinder. Beneath that nontraditional, asymmetrical hood scoop were 175 standard horses—that's right, 175 horsepower from only 140 cubic inches. Dearborn's own 5.0-liter High Output (HO) engine needed twice as many cylinders and 182 more cubes to make that much power for the 1983 Mustang GT, leaving some witnesses wondering what the SVO guys knew that others didn't. First off, they recognized that a clunky carburetor was no way to feed a true high-performance machine; more advanced fuel-delivery technology was available to help make a screamer out of any engine, regardless of cylinder count.

Calling the engine a "techno-freak's fantasy in living metal," *Motor Trend*'s Kevin Smith described the SVO Mustang as "Ford's future think car," or "Future Boss." "What Ford is saying with this car is, okay, we used to get horsepower by dumping loads of air and fuel down huge cylinder bores, but the way to do it now is with on-demand force feeding and sophisticated electronic management of a smaller, lighter powerplant."

1984 FORD MUSTANG SVO

Type: water-cooled SOHC inline four-cylinder

Construction: cast-iron block and cylinder head

Main bearings: five

Bore and stroke: 3.78x3.13 inches

Displacement: 140 cubic inches/2.3 liters

Valves: two valves per cylinder

Camshaft: belt-driven single overhead unit

Compression: 8.0:1

Induction: Intercooled Garrett AiResearch T3 turbocharger with 14-psi maximum boost

Ignition: EEC IV electronic controls

Horsepower: 175 at 4,400 rpm

Torque: 210 at 3,000 rpm

Ford first turbocharged its 2.3-liter four-cylinder in 1979, making this engine a Mustang option that year. A much-improved force-fed four (shown here) then debuted in 1983 for the new Thunderbird Turbo Coupe.

Along with 175 turbocharged horses, Ford's 1984 SVO Mustang also came standard with a Hurst-shifted five-speed manual transmission, Koni shock absorbers, four-wheel disc brakes, and 16-inch aluminum wheels.

Force feeding the SVO four was a Garrett AiResearch T3 turbocharger that produced maximum boost of 14 psi at around 4,200 rpm. Ford's first turbocharged engine had appeared in 1979 as a Mustang option, and in this case an exhaust-driven turbo fed boost to a typical two-barrel carburetor. Output for this 2.3-liter four-cylinder was 140 horsepower. A much improved turbo four then debuted midway through 1983 for the aptly named Thunderbird Turbo Coupe, which featured more precise port fuel injection in place of a carburetor to help raise the output ante to 145 horsepower.

Electronic-controlled fuel injection had debuted in Ford Motor Company ranks for the 1980 Lincoln Versailles; this after the corporation had introduced its electronic engine control (EEC) system for carbureted engines in 1978. An improved EEC II appeared in 1979, followed by the EEC III the following year. The latter was found on carbureted engines as well as Lincoln's 5.0-liter V-8 with its centralized fuel injection. Next was Ford's superior EEC IV computer control with its onboard self-diagnostic system in 1984.

The EEC IV system on the SVO four-cylinder for 1984 not only made sure the port injectors delivered fuel as efficiently as possible, it also worked the turbocharger's waste gate, which was mechanically controlled on Ford's other turbo fours. Also included in the electronic control system was a switch on the dash that changed air/fuel metering calibrations, depending on which grade of fuel was pumped in, regular or premium. This switch limited boost to 10 psi whenever regular unleaded was chosen.

Topping off the SVO engine was an air-to-air intercooler that lowered the temperature of the compressed atmosphere heading into the intake manifold. Cooler air is denser, and denser air is key to more efficient combustion. Intercooling, in turn, was key to squeezing so many more horses from those four little cylinders. But it couldn't compensate for the one downside produced by all turbochargers: the lag time experienced as exhaust pressures built up to drive the impeller that spun up to compress the incoming air. Though turbo lag has been minimized in today's boosted engines, it was an inherent hiccup that SVO Mustang drivers had to overlook back in 1984 to best appreciate this particular brand of performance.

And a balanced brand it was. Estimated fuel economy was 21 miles per gallon in the city, an appealing 32 on the highway—this from a pony car that also could downright get it. According to a *Car and Driver* road test, the 0–60 run went by in 7.5 seconds, the quarter-mile in 15.5 clicks. Not bad at all, certainly so for an engine that, like all four-cylinders, couldn't possibly compete with its V-8 brethren in the torque-churning arena. Maximum torque output was 210 ft-lb at 3,000 rpm, compared to 245 ft-lb for the Mustang GT's 5.0-liter V-8.

The SVO attraction didn't end beneath the hood. Overall impressions were enhanced by a biplane spoiler in back and ground effects added just in front of the rear wheels. Throw in a Hurst-shifted five-speed manual transmission, Koni gas-charged shocks absorbers, quick-ratio steering, four-wheel disc brakes, and 16-inch aluminum wheels, and the sum of the parts equaled a GT street racer that even European drivers could love.

Americans, however, couldn't quite warm up to what at the time amounted to one of the best all-around performers in Mustang history. That performance received even more of a boost in 1985, after horsepower was increased to 205 thanks to a revised intake, improved turbo housing, a longer duration cam, larger Bosch injectors, and less restrictive exhausts with twin tailpipes trailing the single catalytic converter. Yet buyers still remained cool. Ford canceled the SVO Mustang in 1986 after 9,844 were sold during the short three-year run.

That the SVO Mustang came and went in such a rush wasn't necessarily the car's fault. Ford officials later admitted that making muscle, not marketing it, was the SVO's forte. A better-balanced business approach would come along in the 1990s to promote an even better breed of hot-to-trot Mustang, this one with traditional, Yankee-friendly V-8 power.

This time the initials would be "SVT," Special Vehicle Team to you.

Ford built only 9,844 SVO Mustangs from 1984 to 1986. The last of the line is shown here.

A revamped intake, improved turbocharger, longer-duration cam, and larger injectors helped increase the SVO four-cylinder's output to 205 horsepower in 1985. The 1986 edition (shown here) then fell back to 200 horses.

Buick's hottest 3800 V-6 appeared in 1987 for the ASC/McLaren GNX, a black beauty built for one year only. Output for the turbocharged 3.8-liter GNX V-6 was 276 horsepower.

CHAPTER 22

Bad to the Bone: Buick ASC/McLaren GNX V-6

As most of us know, Chevrolet's small-block V-8 celebrated its 50th anniversary in 2005. Naming General Motors' second-longest running engine, however, is not so easy. Anyone?

Buick's long-running V-6 legacy dates back to 1961, when General Motors introduced the industry's first aluminum V-8. In 1962, this 215-cubic-inch V-8 was cut down into a 90-degree V-6 for both Buick and Oldsmobile. *Steve and Pattie Constable photo, courtesy General Motors*

Try the 3800 V-6, a potent little powerplant that traces its ancestry back to 1962—or 1961 if you want to get technical. Though this legacy appears to be winding down as we speak, no tears should be shed; the years have all been good ones, and even greater V-6 technology is emerging at GM to pick up whenever this old faithful engine leaves off. During its long career, the 3800 V-6 has seen service throughout GM's divisions in seemingly countless models. But its highest times easily came when packaged by Buick, the firm responsible for its conception.

In 1961, Buick became the first American automaker to offer an aluminum V-8, a 215-cubic-inch engine created to help keep weight down for the company's new downsized Special. The Big Three had just discovered compacts, and the aluminum V-8 led Buick's attempt to enter this field, albeit at a much higher level than the likes of Chevrolet's Corvair. But high production costs helped scuttle this lightweight engine after only three years.

In its stead came America's first mass-market V-6, introduced for 1962. Buick engineers created this milestone by following Pontiac, which had simply sawed its V-8 in half to produce an economical inline four-cylinder for 1961. Buick did similar cutting on its 215-ci V-8, lopping off only two cylinders to produce a 90-degree V-6. Originally displacing 198 cubic inches, this economical engine was recast in iron for simplicity's sake. Displacement went up to 225 cubic inches in 1964, but then V-6 demand went down and cancellation followed by the end of 1967.

The entire manufacturing line was then sold to Kaiser Jeep, which moved the works to its plant in Toledo, Ohio, where the former Buick V-6 found a new home in the CJ-5 Jeep and Jeepster. The plot thickened further when American Motors acquired Kaiser Jeep in 1969, after which time AMC officials quietly nudged the GM-born V-6 out of the picture, canceling it a second time in 1972.

Enter Buick, again. Spurred on by the fuel crisis of 1973, the folks in Flint once more began considering small engines for smaller cars. But why tool up for totally new equipment when proven parts were collecting dust in Toledo? GM officials approached AMC with an offer to buy back the old V-6 line, and they struck a deal in the spring of 1974. Back in Michigan in 1975, the familiar friend was enlarged to 231 cubic inches (3.8 liters) and installed in Buick's new compact Skyhawk, as well as the Apollo, Skylark, and midsized Century. Pontiac and Oldsmobile began offering the engine in similar models.

Refinements included a switch to an even-fire design for 1977 and optional turbocharging the following year. Turbo engines were nothing new around Detroit, but Buick engineers were able to take the technology to new heights. Most successful among a series of too-cool-for-school turbocharged V-6 models, the bad, black Regal-based Grand National was built from 1984 to 1987.

Early force-fed V-6 Buicks used conventional carburetors. But then Ron Kociba's Turbo Engine Group in Buick Engineering unveiled a high-tech, computer-controlled, sequential fuel-injected V-6 for 1984. Output was a healthy 200 horsepower. Two years later, the Turbo Group's Ron Yuille developed an air-to-air intercooler for the boosted V-6, helping raise the power ante to 235 horses. The 3.8-liter Buick turbo engine hit 245 horsepower in 1987, the last year for the rear-driven Regal.

A major refitting for 1988 resulted in a new name for the 3.8-liter Buick V-6, the "3800." Buick recast the basic structure to better align the cylinders with the even-fire crankshaft, and additional upgrades included lightweight pistons, roller lifters, tubular exhausts, and a balance

The GNX was the result of a joint venture between General Motors, McLaren, and the American Sunroof Company. ASC (now known as American Specialty Cars) was founded in 1965 by Heinz Prechter, pictured at the driver's door of a 1987 GNX with his crew in the background. Prechter died in July 2001. He was inducted into the Automotive Hall of Fame in October 2004.

Only 547 GNX Buicks, all painted black and fitted with fender flares, were built for 1987 to mark the end of the road for the company's Grand National line.

A McLaren-modified Garrett T3 turbocharger supplied 15 pounds of boost. It was mated to a custom-built Garrett intercooler.

shaft to reduce vibration. A supercharged 3800, rated at 205 horsepower, appeared for Buick's Park Avenue Ultra in 1991. And when the sensational '95 Riviera debuted, its standard engine was the newly updated "Series II" 3800 V-6, rated at 205 horsepower. The Riviera offered an optional supercharged 3800, producing 225 horses. In 2005, Pontiac's Grand Prix GTP Comp G featured a blown 3800 V-6 that made 260 horsepower.

But easily the best punch packed by the 3.8-liter bunch came back in 1987 in the form of the GNX, a special-edition Grand National built by Buick with the help of an ASC/McLaren joint venture. In keeping with the Grand National tradition, all 547 ASC/McLaren GNX models were painted black, and they were adorned with functional fender vents (to let underhood heat escape) and flared bodywork. Those flared fenders housed fat Goodyear Gatorbacks on sexy 16-inch alloy wheels. And underneath was a revised rear suspension with a longitudinal ladder bar (in place of the stock upper control arms) and a lateral Panhard rod.

McLaren Engines and the American Sunroof Company first teamed up in 1983 to produce a customized Capri for Mercury. Founded in 1965 by Heinz Prechter, ASC made its name by creating several convertible conversions for various companies and later was responsible for the retractable hardtop on Chevrolet's SSR pickup. In 2004, the ASC translation officially changed to "American Specialty Cars" to better reflect the company's wide-ranging engineering experience.

Buick representatives met with ASC/McLaren officials in May 1986 to discuss plans for the GNX, which Buick Chief Engineer Dave Sharpe hoped would serve as a sensational sendoff for the Grand National bloodline. Buick General Manager Donald Hackworth gave the project a go-ahead in July, and nine prototypes were built before actual production commenced. During testing, one of those prototypes rocketed through the quarter-mile in less than 13.4 seconds. In most minds, the turbocharged Grand National already represented the 1980s' hottest muscle car—clearly the even-nastier GNX would be going where no contemporary could possible go.

A McLaren-modified 3.8-liter turbo V-6 powered the GNX. That modified powerplant would've put most high-performance V-8s of the 1960s and 1970s to shame. Buick advertised the little bomb at 276 horsepower, and that was a net rating. Prior to 1972, Detroit used less-accurate gross ratings that didn't reflect power losses incurred as the horses made their way from combustion chamber to the road. The GNX's rating represented real power at the rear wheels, power that you could use with a vengeance. Also note that those 276 ponies came from only 231 cubes—not until recent times has an American car offered such an awesome horsepower-per-cubic-inch ratio.

Buick supplied McLaren with basic 3.8-liter turbo short blocks, which used stronger pistons and more lubricant volume (5 quarts instead of 4) than their naturally aspirated V-6 cousins. McLaren added a modified Garrett T-3 turbocharger with a ceramic impeller, drag-reducing seals, and an oversized exhaust housing. The latter helped improve high-rpm performance by speeding spent gases on their way, while the ceramic impeller helped the turbo spool up faster, which in turn reduced lag as full boost (15 psi) arrived in rapid fashion. Coupled with the T-3 unit was a custom Garrett intercooler created especially for the GNX application. McLaren people also made PROM (programmable read-only memory) adjustments in the 3.8 turbo's ECM (electronic control module) to maximize performance and efficiency, and to keep close tabs on the demands put on the GNX's four-speed Turbo Hydra-matic 200-4R automatic transmission.

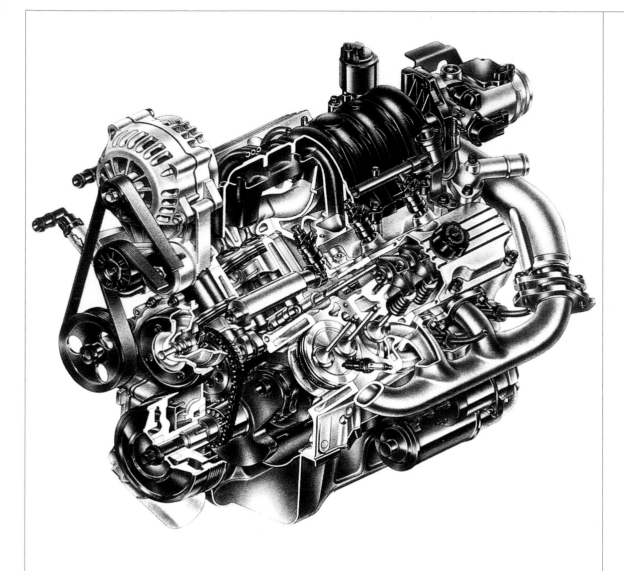

The revamped series II 3800-series V-6 debuted along with Buick's sensational Riviera in 1995. Output was 205 horsepower.

A supercharged 3800 V-6, rated at 225 horsepower, became an option for the 1995 Riviera.

Buick's sequential fuel injection system, featuring Bosch injectors, shot the juice into the Garrett-pressurized airflow. A modified system that included dual pipes and mufflers behind the single catalytic converter handled exhaust chores. Those low-restriction mufflers gave the GNX a growl that couldn't be missed. Completing the package was an ASC-installed transmission cooler, located in front of the radiator.

Once on the streets in 1987, the bad-to-the-bone Buick GNX couldn't be beat. *Car and Driver* called it "an axe-wielding barbarian laying waste to everything in its path." Horsepower hounds who thought they'd seen the last of Detroit's factory hot rods simply said "cool."

When introduced in 1990, the Dodge Viper's V-10 produced 400 horsepower. Appearing here is the 450-horsepower rendition, introduced along with the GTS coupe in 1996.

CHAPTER 23

Savage Snake: Dodge Viper V-10

Dodge's venomous Viper was still just a prototype when it paced the 75th

running of the Indianapolis 500 in May 1991.

More than six months away from its actual

regular-production release, this slithering

snake was rushed in at the last minute as a

substitute at the Brickyard.

1990 DODGE VIPER

Type: water-cooled OHV 90-degree V-10

Construction: aluminum block and cylinder heads

Main bearings: six

Bore and stroke: 4.00x3.88 inches

Displacement: 488 cubic inches

Valves: two per cylinder

Compression: 9.1:1

Induction: sequential multiport fuel injection

Exhaust: cast-steel tubular exhausts, dual sidepipes

Ignition: electronic control

Horsepower: 400 at 5,200 rpm

Torque: 450 at 3,600 rpm

A Viper concept car was unveiled at the North American International Auto Show in Detroit in 1989. At the wheel is Robert Lutz, then president of Chrysler. Behind are (left to right) Tom Gale, vice president of product design; Cobra man Carroll Shelby; and Francois Castaing, vice president of vehicle engineering.

The first choice—a 1991 Dodge Stealth—was pooh-poohed, most notably by United Auto Workers members, who would be building the Viper at Chrysler's New Mack Avenue Process Development Center in Detroit. Though Chrysler-designed, the sporty Stealth was manufactured by the corporation's Far East partner, Mitsubishi, and in the red-white-and-blue opinion of Indianapolis-based UAW Region 3 Director William Oros, there was no way a "foreign car" would ever pace the 500.

"There is a strong feeling of patriotism in this country these days," explained Chrysler Marketing Vice President John Damoose in February 1991 while announcing the switch from the Stealth pace car to Viper. "It is almost as if America has awakened and said, 'Our technology is as good as the rest of the world, and we're proud of it.'" Of course, the first Gulf War in Iraq had a lot to do with that patriotic fervor, but why point out the obvious? Instead, Damoose did a little chest pounding.

"The Viper is a symbol of the can-do attitude and the technical innovation of the American auto industry," he continued. "And there can be no doubt about its heritage. It was born here, designed here, developed, engineered, and will be built here. That's what America wants in an Indy 500 pace car right now."

Indianapolis Motor Speedway (IMS) officials made the Viper's pinch-hit appearance possible by waving its requirement that three identical pace car candidates be provided by a manufacturer at least two months prior to the race. Instead, the one Viper prototype, driven by Carroll Shelby, hit the Bricks in May 1991, relegating various Stealth models to Indy 500 "Official Car" duties.

UAW officials were tickled pink about the switch. "We think that's entirely appropriate for this premier American sporting event," said Oros.

Could it get more American than Viper? Big and heavy (for a roadster). Rear wheel drive. A mondo motor up front, churning out gobs of horsepower. An oversexed body, bulging in all the right (and some wrong) places. Chevrolet's Corvette will always claim the title of "America's sports car," but it became clear in January 1992 that a serious challenger would be here to stay. And if the message wasn't clear enough, there was a plaque in the glove box explaining that this new kid on the block was "designed, developed, and manufactured in the Motor City by Team Viper."

That team's coach was Chrysler President Robert Lutz, one of Detroit's last great car guys. As the story goes, Lutz just happened to hook up with design VP Tom Gale in a Highland Park hallway in February 1988, and in a quick conversation Lutz mentioned his thoughts about building a modern-day Shelby Cobra. As luck would have it, Gale's people had already started drawing up just such a machine late in 1987. Clay models quickly followed, and before anyone knew it, Dodge had a concept vehicle wowing the crowd at Detroit's North American International Auto Show in January 1989. Next, as *Automobile* magazine's Robert Cumberford explained, came "the kind of response every manufacturer dreams about: people waving checkbooks and demanding early delivery."

Somewhat amazingly, much of that original concept carried over into the finished product, which Lutz and Team Viper consultant Carroll Shelby introduced to the press at the Detroit Auto Show in 1992. Underneath was a road-hugging chassis independently sprung in back. On top was bold, seething bodywork made of fiberglass. And the name on the new Dodge was "RT/10," for "road and track, 10 cylinders."

Much has been uttered over the years since about the Viper's truck engine. But most wags learned right away that they'd better say that with a smile. Yes, the Viper's all-aluminum V-10

Beneath the GTS Viper's new closed body was a redesigned chassis and 450 newfound horses. Convenient roll-up windows and exterior door handles also debuted with the GTS.

was a spin-off from Dodge truck developments, yet how could anyone argue with 400 horsepower and 450 ft-lb of torque? Right out of the box, the first Viper roadster was able to run from rest to 60 miles per hour in about 4 ticks, and the quarter-mile went by in a tad less than 13 seconds. Know any truck that fast? Or for that matter any Corvette? Not even Chevy's high-tech ZR-1, built from 1990 to 1995, could compete with the awesome RT/10.

The RT/10's power source was another Bob Lutz idea. Running up against Chevrolet big-block pickups in the 1980s, the Dodge Ram truck could only muster a tired 5.9-liter (360 cubic inches) small block, and this mill couldn't possibly match the torque its rivals were churning out. To get back in the utility vehicle race, Lutz proposed recasting the 5.9-liter V-8 with two extra cylinders to open the door for more power potential.

But wasn't a V-10 almost impossible to balance? Along with that, it was known that the optimum angle between banks (to minimize those inherent vibrations) in a 10-cylinder power-plant was 72 degrees. The 5.9-liter engine was a 90-degree V-8, meaning of course that its V-10 cousin would also follow in this format. In most opinions, not even truck drivers would be comfortable with all the expected moving and shaking provided by the proposed monster.

Snake-like tubular exhausts keep spent gases flowing out of the Viper V-10.

Engineers calmed this beast considerably by, among other things, creating an uneven firing pattern for those 10 cylinders. As *Motor Trend*'s Don Sherman explained, "The interval between power pulses alternates between 54 and 90 degrees of crankshaft rotation. Primary forces are in balance, but a secondary lateral shake exists, which, according to a Chrysler engineer, is smaller in magnitude than the typical V-6 disturbance."

When introduced for Dodge's 1994 truck line, the resulting V-10 featured a cylinder block and heads made of cast iron. For the 1992 Viper, however, this heavyweight was trimmed down by 100 pounds or so by using aluminum for the block and cylinder heads. Well versed in exotic aluminum engines, Lamborghini Engineering was invited to help make the lightened V-10 a reality. Further weight-conscious touches included magnesium valve covers. Cast-iron cylinder sleeves went into that aluminum block, which featured a heavy-duty ladder-type main bearing girdle housed with an extended deep-skirt lower end. A 4.00-inch bore was matched up to a 3.88-inch stroke to equal 488 cubic inches, or 8.0 liters. Compression was 9.1:1.

From there, the Viper V-10 was very much a meat-and-potatoes mill: pushrods, two valves in each combustion chamber, sequential multipoint fuel injection. But everything worked well together, from that tuned intake to those cast-steel tubular headers feeding spent gases to a pair of shin-burning Walker sidepipes. If there was one noticeable knock, it involved that exhaust system, which in some opinions gave away the Viper engine's pickup roots. According to *AutoWeek*'s Matt DeLorenzo, the original RT/10 roadster sounded like "a UPS truck at idle."

"Because of the uneven firing pulses, the exhaust note is sort of a macho staccato chugga-chugga with a slight wheeze," added *Road & Track*'s Ron Sessions. Maybe so, but most drivers couldn't care less once all 10 cylinders really start singing. "The exhaust note sounds more serpentine than spirited, but the Viper hasn't yet undergone voice training," explained Don Sherman. "That procedure may not be necessary; when the accelerator is mashed, the howl of protest by the rear pair of Goodyear Eagle GTs will doubtlessly drown out all lesser sounds."

Such comments began fading away after the last sidepiped Viper was built in 1995. Power increases, too, helped critics forget all about the V-10's different exhaust note. First came 415 horsepower for the RT/10 in 1996 and 450 horses that same year for the classic GTS coupe with its Shelby-style white-striped blue body. Output hit 500 horsepower when the latest Viper rendition, the SRT-10, was introduced for 2003. Displacement that year went up to 8.3 liters (505 cubic inches), and this V-10 was up to 510 horsepower for the 2006 SRT-10.

But Chevrolet now has a new Z06 Corvette, a 505-horse bomb, able to run neck and neck with Dodge's long-running king of the American performance ring. According to an *AutoWeek* comparison test, the latest Viper can go 0–60 in 4.2 seconds, the quarter-mile in 12.37 seconds at 117.3 miles per hour. The corresponding numbers for the '06 Z06 are 3.91 and 12 flat at 121.7.

Maybe it's time the Dodge boys considered a V-12.

Viper updates over the years included dropping the exposed side exhausts after 1995. The GTS coupe joined the topless RT-10 in 1996, and power for the latter model went up to 415 horsepower that year. Shown here is one of the 837 GTS coupes built for 1998.

Ford's Special Vehicle Team added a supercharger and intercooler to the already hot 4.6-liter dual-overhead-cam V-8 in 2003, resulting in what insiders called "The Terminator." Output for this blown mill was 390 horsepower.

CHAPTER 24 Cobra Venom:

Ford SVT 4.6-liter "Terminator" V-8

"Biggest bang for the buck"—Chevrolet's Camaro and Ford's Mustang battled for this unofficial honor year in, year out during the 1980s. Which car offered the most performance per dollar was a close call in those days, but then Chevy engineers dropped the Corvette's new-and-improved LT1 V-8 into the 1993 Camaro Z28.

A single-overhead-cam 4.6-liter V-8 debuted as the Mustang GT's standard power source in 1996. A DOHC counterpart became the SVT Cobra's (shown here) heart and soul that year.

At 275 horsepower, the 5.7-liter LT1 easily overshadowed Ford's venerable High Output (HO) 5.0 V-8, which that year was rerated down to 205 horsepower after operating at its peak of 225 horses from 1987 to 1992. No worries, though, thought the Mustang faithful; a radically redesigned pony car was waiting in the wings at the time, and the Blue Oval guys surely were going to retaliate, right?

Wrong, at least at first. After spending $700 million on both the car and its assembly plant, Ford started building its truly new 1994 Mustang in October 1993. Reportedly 1,330 of the car's 1,850 parts were making their debut in 1994, yet there was still something missing. Next to nothing new was found beneath the hood, where a 215-horse 5.0-liter HO V-8 kept the next-generation GT running strong, but not strong enough to catch up with its Z28 rival, a disappointing fact some critics simply couldn't overlook. "For at least six years now, Mustang was a terrific engine in search of a better car," wrote *AutoWeek*'s John Clor. "Now it's a better car in search of even more power."

Fortunately, that search ended two years later as the aging "five-oh" HO finally was traded for Ford's thoroughly modern "modular motor," a 4.6-liter V-8 wearing a chain-driven single overhead cam (SOHC) in each cylinder head. Modular V-8 roots dated back to 1987, the idea being to develop a basic engine layout that could be easily morphed into various forms, sharing many main components in the process. Early mod motors were of SOHC design, featuring aluminum heads and two valves per cylinder, with the first of these 4.6-liter V-8s showing up (at 190 horsepower, 210 with optional dual exhausts) for the Lincoln Town Car in 1991. Two years later, the Mk. VIII Lincoln coupe debuted with an all-aluminum, dual-overhead-cam (DOHC), 32-valve, 4.6-liter V-8 rated at 280 horsepower. The use of four cams and four valves per cylinder each represented Ford Motor Company regular-production firsts, and yet another milestone came when the DOHC mod motor (mounted transversely) became a front-driver for the redesigned Lincoln Continental in 1995. All modular V-8s, regardless of cam and valve count or constitution (iron or aluminum), have been produced at Ford's engine plant in Romeo, Michigan.

Standard equipment for the 1996 Mustang GT was an electronically injected, 215-horsepower, 4.6-liter SOHC V-8, an engine that was both lighter and more durable than the 5.0-liter, as well as smoother running. And, according to Mustang vehicle line director Janine Bay, Ford's mod motor also transformed the GT "from a good to a great car." Bay continued, "We've opened up the usable rpm range, providing a whole lot more fun and power through the entire rpm band."

"What the 4.6-liter engines bring to customers is a new sense of performance and excitement," added John Hasse, supervisor of Mustang V-8 engine systems. "Buyers of the 1996 Mustangs will feel the old excitement of the original mid-1960s pony cars, but they'll also appreciate the benefits of the mid-1990s technology."

More benefits arrived in 1998 as output was boosted to 225 horsepower, then some serious tweaking upped the ante to 260 horses for the 1999 GT. But even more impressive was the mod motor developed by Ford's Special Vehicle Team.

SVT was created in 1991 to pick up where Ford's Special Vehicle Operations (SVO) had left off back in the 1980s. The new group's job was to build and market special high-performance versions of Ford products, and that they did. Over the next 10 years or so, the Mustang, Contour, Focus, and F-150 half-ton truck all were treated to the SVT touch. First came the Lightning pickup and Mustang Cobra coupe in 1993, with the latter relying on a warmed-over 235-horsepower 5.0-liter V-8, followed by a 240-horse 5.0-liter for 1994 (when a convertible model joined the lineup) and 1995.

Then, like its GT cousin, the SVT Cobra traded pushrods for overhead cams in 1996 but used four instead of two. This all-aluminum, 32-valve, 4.6-liter V-8 also made nearly 50 percent more power than its cast-iron, two-valves-per-cylinder, SOHC regular-production running mate. Output for the DOHC Cobra V-8 was a whopping 305 horses, more than enough muscle to blast the 1996 SVT Mustang through the quarter-mile in less than 14 seconds. The most venomous Cobra yet was a dozen miles per hour faster (152 miles per hour) on the top end than its 5.0-liter predecessor and a good half-second quicker (5.9 clicks) running 0–60. And talk about biggest bang for the buck: Discounting foreign exotics, there were only three other convertibles running around American roads in 1996 fitted with DOHC engines producing more than 300 horsepower, and all three cost more than $65,000. At $28,080, the '96 SVT Cobra ragtop was a steal in comparison.

Ford officials, however, had to shell out $3.4 million to create a special assembly line at the Romeo engine works to carefully manufacture the 4.6-liter Cobra V-8. The first of its kind in the mass-production world, this hands-on line, in the words of Romeo Plant Manager Harvey Byrne, allowed Ford "the opportunity to build specialty engines at low volumes, cost effectively and at high quality." Each engine was hand-built by a two-person team that moved through 10 work stations, where the parts and tools for the various assembly processes were waiting. At the end of the line, the two technicians then fixed an autographed plaque to their baby to let the world know who the proud papas and mamas were.

"This is the only place in the Ford group, apart from Aston Martin, where employees put their signature on an engine," explained Byrne. "This is a mark of pride in the product and a commitment to the quality with which it is built." Hand-built, hand-signed V-8s remained a proud tradition until the last SVT Cobra was released in 2004.

Ten years and more than 100,000 specialty machines after it first began turning Ford buyers' heads, SVT celebrated a decade in business in 2003 with a special anniversary model based on its popular Mustang variant. Available for both Cobra coupes and convertibles in 2003, this 10th Anniversary package consisted of appropriate logos on the deck lid and floor mats, leather interior appointments in black with red inserts, and a carbon-fiber look for the steering wheel, shifter boot, and brake handle. But the main attraction came beneath the hood.

2003–2004 FORD SVT COBRA

Type: water-cooled DOHC 90-degree V-8

Construction: cast-iron block, aluminum cylinder heads

Main bearings: five, with fully counter-weighted forged crankshaft

Bore and stroke: 3.6x3.6 inches

Displacement: 4.6 liters (280 cubic inches)

Valves: four per cylinder

Camshaft: chain-driven dual overhead units

Compression: 8.5:1

Induction: sequential electronic fuel injection with Eaton Generation IV Roots-type super-charger (8.0-psi maximum boost)

Exhaust: dual stainless-steel pipes

Ignition: distributor-less coil-on-plug

Horsepower: 390 at 6,000 rpm

Torque: 390 at 3,500 rpm

Ford's new-for-1996 DOHC Cobra V-8 (center) poses with two other legendary Blue Oval powerplants: the Boss 429 (left) and 427 SOHC "Cammer" (right). Output for the 1996 Cobra V-8 was 305 horsepower.

All 4.6-liter SVT Cobra V-8s were hand-assembled by a two-person team, who then signed off on their work by autographing a valve cover on each engine.

All SVT Cobra Mustangs for 2003, anniversary model or not, were powered by a sensationally supercharged and intercooled 4.6-liter DOHC V-8 that pumped out 390 seriously snorting horses, making it a "true performance value," according to SVT Sales and Marketing Manager Tom Scarpello. As Scarpello explained, "The next closest competitor to meet or exceed the SVT Cobra's 390 horsepower costs more than $50,000." Base prices for the 2003 supercharged Cobra coupe and convertible were $34,750 and $38,995, respectively.

Code-named the "Terminator" in house at SVT, the supercharged Cobra owed its existence to developments first made beneath the Lightning pickup's hood in 1999. Introduced in 1993, SVT's original F-150 Lightning had been fitted with a 240-horse, 351-cubic-inch V-8, and this package rolled on up through 1995 before temporarily retiring. When it returned for 1999, an all-new, way-cool Lightning featured a 5.4-liter aluminum-head SOHC mod motor topped by a Roots-type Eaton supercharger. Output was 360 horsepower for the second-generation SVT pickup, which could haul ass from 0–60 in a tidy 6.2 seconds, inspiring *Car and Driver* to claim that Ford had built "the world's fastest pickup," an unofficial tag that Ford later got certified in 2003.

In the meantime, SVT people created even more thunder with the Lightning in 2001, upping the Eaton-blown 5.4-liter V-8's output to 380 horsepower. A few enlarged pieces (mass airflow meter and air intake opening) and a higher-flow intake manifold helped produce those extra ponies. On the street, all that power translated into 5.8 seconds for the 0–60 run, 13.9 ticks for the quarter-mile. On a test track in 2003, a stock supercharged Lightning hit 147 miles per hour, a feat that the Guinness World Records people officially acknowledged that August as being the fastest a "production pickup truck" ever ran. But the Lightning wasn't the only SVT vehicle to make its mark that year.

"Every once in a while, a car comes along that really shakes up the status quo," explained Tom Scarpello. "Since the '64 1/2 Mustang, there have been a number of Mustangs that set the standard for performance when they were introduced. The 2003 SVT Cobra is the new benchmark, and proudly carries on the tradition of Mustang performance leadership."

Along with its superb chassis—which featured, among other things, huge Goodyear Eagle tires on 17x9 rims and independent suspension in back, a Cobra standard since 1999—the 2003 Cobra contained that awesome Terminator V-8, a product of SVT Chief Engineer John Coletti's ongoing pursuit of ultimate performance. According to Cobra Program Manager Tom Bochenek, Coletti decided that the existing 4.6-liter V-8 had gone about as far as it could go with natural aspiration. Bolting on the force-fed Lightning's blower simply represented the next logical choice.

"We had some pretty successful SVT Mustangs (before 2003)," said Coletti, "but the whole idea is to improve. That's what we're committed to, and the number one thing our customers want is enhanced performance. The supercharged engine allowed us to go where we needed to go—to give our customers a whole lot more car than ever before."

Initial plans called for an Eaton M-90 supercharger, but it was too small for the 32-valve engine's demands. The Lightning's larger M-112 blower proved to be just the ticket for the 4.6, with the installation requiring a relocated air inlet (moved from the top in the truck to the back for the Cobra) to clear the Mustang's much lower hood. Key to the Eaton unit's efficient operation was an air-to-water intercooler, which relied on its own independent coolant reservoir, instead of borrowing fluid from the engine.

Additional upgrades included revised aluminum cylinder heads, a longer duration cam, and an expected drop in compression (from 9.85:1 to 8.5:1) to compensate for the supercharger's extra boost (7.5 to 8 psi). Coletti's people also didn't trust the aluminum cylinder block to handle the demands made by all that newfound blown performance, so they switched to a conventional cast-iron block. Special forged pistons with dished tops went inside those iron bores, and they were tied to the existing Cobra V-8's forged-steel crank by eight super-heavy-duty Manley H-beam forged connecting rods. Another racing parts firm, ARP, supplied the extra strong rod bolts.

An increased-capacity fuel pump was added to ensure ample flow to larger, freer-flowing injectors (39 pounds per hour, compared to the existing 24 pounds per hour). The mass air meter too predictably grew, from 80 to 90 millimeters. A revised two-piece intake manifold was required for the supercharger application, while the throttle body (with twin 57-millimeter bores) was a carryover.

Working together, these parts helped make for as wild a ride ever delivered by Ford's pony car. "It has power that gives gratification on demand," bragged Coletti. "When you open the throttle, it just goes!" SVT tests resulted in a top end of 155 miles per hour for the so-called Terminator Mustang. According to *Car and Driver*, only 4.5 seconds were needed to reach 60 miles per hour from rest. And *Muscle Mustangs and Fast Fords* magazine claimed a 12.67-second burst through the quarter-mile, topping out at 110.11 miles per hour. Clearly, Coletti wasn't kidding.

The blown Cobra carried over into 2004 but didn't make the jump into the Mustang's next generation for 2005. John Coletti retired at the end of 2004, leaving Ford's Special Vehicle Team without its driving force. And, as these words go to press in 2006, it appears that, if SVT does live on, it will do so only in name alone. Another of Coletti's toys, the outrageous GT, will survive for now, as will the Shelby Cobra GT500 concept, the latter apparently serving as the SVT Cobra's successor. But the old familiar team itself will never work together again—pity.

Apparently that Terminator code name carried more significance than Coletti and crew intended.

True to their name, the Manley connecting rods (upper left) used inside the Terminator V-8 made their standard 4.6-liter counterparts look wimpy in comparison.

Every bit as bodacious as the 1970 Boss 429 (background), Ford's SVT Cobra Mustang marked its 10th anniversary in 2003 with newfound supercharged power to go along with various dress-up pieces.

Displacing a familiar 427 cubic inches (7.0 liters), Chevrolet's LS7 V-8 produces a whopping 505 horsepower, second in America only to the 2006 Dodge Viper's 510-horse V-10. *David Kimble cutaway, courtesy General Motors*

CHAPTER 25

Fifty Years and Still Running Strong: Chevrolet LS7 V-8

Most of us would surely sell our souls to stay in such fine shape into our 50s. At an age when many of its owners are on their way down the other side of the hill, Chevrolet's indefatigable small-block V-8 is still running strong.

With a $66,000 suggested sticker, Chevrolet's new 2006 Z06 Corvette easily ranks as the world's best performance buy. Top end is just short of 200 miles per hour, while quarter-mile performance registers at 11.7 seconds. Rest to 60 miles per hour requires a scant 3.7 ticks.

Of course, Chevy's latest, greatest small block is by no means the same V-8 that started it all in 1955, but we can squint our eyes and pretend, just as General Motors people have been doing since they first started regenerating the bloodline back in the 1990s. Think of it this way: today's Chevrolet V-8 probably has more in common with its earlier self than Cher does with the young woman who married Sonny.

As its "Gen IV" tag implies, Chevrolet's newest small block belongs to the latest of four generations. Basically an upgraded, bored-out Gen III V-8, the 6.0-liter Gen IV made its first big public splash in 2005 as the new sixth-generation (C6) Corvette's heart and soul, wearing the equally new "LS2" RPO label. This all-aluminum, electronically injected wonder was not only the Corvette's most powerful (at 400 horsepower) standard engine ever, it also was fuel efficient, even more so than the 2004 C5's base 350-horse 5.7-liter LS1 V-8. Imagine that: more displacement, more horses, and more miles per gallon. No, this was not a dazzling magic trick, just Chevy engineers doing what they've done for a half-century now.

"The Gen IV is the best example yet of the continuous refinement in performance and efficiency that has been part of the small block's legacy since day one," explained Engineering Chief Sam Winegarden in October 2003, well ahead of the LS2's public unveiling. "(This) long history is one of the reasons the new generation of engines is so powerful and efficient. GM has almost 50 years of experience with its valve-in-head design, and that has provided immeasurable detail for keeping the small block a viable, relevant engine for today and the future."

More than 90 million small blocks have hit the streets during this half-century run, with the retroactively named Gen I group surviving for 36 years before Chevy engineers finally decided a facelift was in order. Electronic fuel injection advances had modernized the first-generation small block during the 1980s, yet beneath that newfangled hardware beat the heart of essentially the same "mouse motor" born in 1955. So it was left to engineer Anil Kulkarni to oversee some serious surgery.

By the time his team was done, very little interchanged between the resulting Gen II LT1 and its 350-cubic-inch predecessor. Block height, bore spacing, and displacement did carry over from Gen I to II. But most everything else was drawn up on a clean sheet of paper, beginning with the iron cylinder block and aluminum heads, which were all recast to incorporate a revised reverse-flow cooling system. Additional changes included trading tuned-port injection (TPI) for a superior multiport fuel injection setup, with the sum of these parts adding up to 300 standard horses for the revitalized 1992 Corvette. The Gen II V-8 remained the C4 Corvette's powerplant up through 1996.

The Gen III small block debuted in 1997, along with the radically redesigned C5 Corvette. Like all small blocks before, the '97 Corvette's new 345-horsepower LS1 V-8 was a traditional pushrod motor with 16 equally traditional valves. It also shared the time-honored "440" block layout (bore centers were 4.40 inches apart) used from the beginning, as well as the familiar 5.7-liter displacement label that dated back to the 1980s. "After all, some things are sacred," said LS1 Engine Program Manager John Juriga. All bets were off from there, however, as the Gen III V-8 represented a real redesign, not just a modernizing makeover.

For starters, the Gen III relied on a different bore/stroke relationship to produce its 5.7 liters—bore was less; stroke was more—to allow more cooling space between skinnier cylinders. The Gen II's reverse-flow cooling system was traded for a conventional layout, as coolant was once again pumped into the block first and then to the heads. But easily the most notable upgrade involved the LS1's all-aluminum construction, a first for a regular-production Chevrolet small block.

At only 107 pounds, the aluminum Gen III cylinder block weighed 53 pounds less than its Gen II forerunner, and the entire engine was 88 pounds lighter. Yet at the same time, the LS1 was much stronger, thanks in part to the block's extensive external stiffening ribs and deep-skirt construction. Unlike typical V-8 blocks that end at the crankshaft's centerline, the LS1 unit extended below the main bearing caps, encasing the crank in a girdle of aluminum for extra durability. That extended skirt also made it possible to cross-bolt the main bearing caps for additional rigidity. LS1 bearing caps used six bolts: four in the conventional vertical location on each side of the crank and one each running through the skirt horizontally into each side of the cap.

On top of that block went aluminum heads that breathed like none before, thanks to replicated ports. As you might guess, these ports were identical in all areas—size, angle, spacing, etc.—and ran almost uninterrupted as straight as possible to the intake valves. Ports in earlier small-block heads varied widely in structure, bending and turning differently with different volumes, and thus their flow characteristics also varied. Keeping flow rates constant from cylinder to cylinder maximizes performance, and that's what the LS1 heads did in strict precision.

Feeding those ports was a sequential electronic port fuel injection system similar to the one used on Corvettes since 1994. Unfamiliar, though, was the glass-fiber composite intake manifold (with specially tuned intake runners) and the drive-by-wire electronic throttle control (ETC), another first. Spark was supplied by a distributor-less ignition system featuring one coil per cylinder. Compression was 10.1:1.

LS1 output was bumped up to 350 horsepower in 2001, but the really big news that year involved the appearance of the Z06 Corvette, a muscled-up, hardtop-only model that instantly reminded Chevy fans of Zora Duntov's original Z06, introduced in 1963. Powering the new Z06 was a warmed-up Gen III V-8 wearing another famous name borrowed from an ancestor: LS6. In 1971, the 425-horse, 454-ci LS6 big block had been the hottest Corvette V-8 offered that year, and the same could be said 30 years later for its small-block namesake, rated at an impressive 385 horsepower.

A recast block, better-breathing heads, stronger pistons, increased compression (to 10.5:1), a lumpier cam, and bigger injectors were just a few of the dozens of improvements that helped transform the LS1 into the LS6. On top, an updated composite intake manifold relied on increased plenum volume and better-flowing runners to reduce turbulence, and this flat-floor intake was added to the LS1 in 2001, resulting in its slight power increase.

Offered only as part of the Z06 package, the LS6 got its own power boost in 2002, this time to a whopping 405 horsepower. Making this jump possible was a free-breathing air box, a low-restriction mass-airflow sensor, a more aggressive cam, revised catalytic converters, and a lightened valvetrain, consisting of sodium-filled exhaust valves and hollow-stem intakes. Z06 power stayed at 405 horses up through 2004, the last year for the C5 platform.

The Z06 didn't reappear in 2005 when the C6 debuted. No worry, though, it returned in stunning fashion for 2006. But first things first: along with the latest best 'Vette yet in 2005 came Chevrolet's latest generation small block, just in time to help celebrate the engine family's 50th anniversary.

As mentioned, the 2005 Corvette's Gen IV V-8 was basically a new-and-improved Gen III small block. Increasing bore from 3.90 inches to 4.00 (stroke stayed at 3.62 inches) bumped the

Early Z06 brochures from Chevrolet showed a badge that read 500 horsepower. They're now collector items after the actual output figure was revised to 505 horses.

Above: The LS7 reportedly is the world's first regular-production pushrod engine capable of confidently revving beyond 7,000 rpm.

Opposite, top: All-aluminum construction became a Chevy small-block trademark when the Gen III V-8 was born in 1997. Pressed-in cylinder sleeves and forged-steel cross-bolted main bearing caps set the LS7 block apart from its LS2 sibling.

Opposite, center: The LS7's aluminum heads are the result of lessons learned on the racetrack. "We adopted some of the latest ideas that have been successful in Nextel Cup and American Le Mans series [competition], including valve centerline positions, valve angles, valve sizes, and rocker arm ratio," said valvetrain design engineer Jim Hicks.

Opposite, bottom: Inside the LS7 are cast-aluminum flat top pistons tied to a forged-steel crank by titanium connecting rods. Compression is 11.0:1.

displacement from 5.7 liters to 6.0—364 cubic inches for you metrically challenged readers. Helping this LS2 V-8 make 400 horsepower was more compression (10.9:1), a higher-lift cam (with higher-rate valve springs), and intake and exhaust flows improved by 15 and 20 percent, respectively. Overall weight, meanwhile, went down by about 15 pounds, courtesy of, among other things, a smaller water pump and thinner-walled exhaust manifolds.

Summed up, these parts equaled surreal performance for the sixth-generation Corvette: 0–60 in 4.2 seconds and a top end of 186 miles per hour, both according to Chevrolet sources. Explaining "why this could be the best sports car in the world," *AutoWeek*'s Wes Raynal couldn't heap enough praise on its power source. "The (LS2) feels like a big block, which was the intention. Acceleration is right now, and the engine pulls and howls beautifully up to the 6,500-rpm redline. And there are just gobs of torque—you could probably get away with a two-speed manual instead of the six-speed: one gear to get off the line, another to take you to 186 mph."

Raves like Raynal's had yet to die down before even more power was added into the C6 equation. Returning for 2006, the new Z06 stands hands down as the most awesome Corvette ever. A direct result of lessons learned while taking the C5-R competition Corvettes to the track, the 2006 Z06 also represents, again according to *AutoWeek*, "the best supercar buy of all time."

"When you compare the Z06 performance stats to other supercars, you see numerous examples where you're getting better performance for one-third the sticker price of some of the competition," explained Chevrolet General Manager Ed Peper. Again according to company tests, the latest Z06 simply scorches the time-honored 0–60 run in 3.7 seconds and completes the quarter-mile in 11.7 ticks at 125 miles per hour. Top end is an unworldly 198 miles per hour. Sure, there are quicker, stronger, faster cars around the world, but none as relatively easy on the wallet as the Z06. Right here in the U.S. of A., Dodge's V-10 Viper makes 510 horsepower—at a base price of $86,995. We don't even need to mention Ford's six-figure GT and its 500-plus horses. Chevrolet's asking price for the 505-horsepower Z06?—a comparatively tidy $66,000.

Included in that bottom line is the longest, most impressive list yet of special features unique to the Z06 package: Bold bodywork that makes the car 3 inches wider than typical C6s. Huge disc brakes (14-inch rotors in front, 13.4 in back) with six-piston calipers at the nose, four-piston units at the tail. Gigantic wheels measuring 18x9.5 inches in front, 19x12 in back. Coolers for all fluids, including power steering. A rear-mounted battery for improved weight distribution. And carbon-fiber composite body panels that help trim overall weight down to a svelte 3,132 pounds.

Last but certainly not least is the Z06's main attraction: the LS7 V-8. Along with being the most powerful small block ever, this all-aluminum screamer also is the largest. Increasing both the Gen IV's bore and stroke (to 4.125 and 4.00 inches, respectively) has produced 427 cubic inches, which translate into 7.0 liters. While its 505 maximum horses arrive at 6,300 rpm, this big, bad small block can confidently rev up to 7,100 rpm, making it one of the world's first regular-production pushrod motors able to regularly breach the seven-grand barrier and survive. The previous Gen IV V-8 extreme was 6,600 rpm for the LS2.

"For a production engine to run at this high of an rpm blurs the lines even more between (pushrod) and overhead-cam design," said Dave Muscaro, assistant chief engineer for small-block engines. "We took a complete systems approach to achieve the high rpm. We have a tight valvetrain design along with some race-inspired materials for the reciprocating components, like titanium intake valves and connecting rods."

Like that lightweight yet bulletproof reciprocating mass, the LS7's cylinder block is also unique, being specially cast to preserve strength while making room for all that bore diameter. Pressed-in cylinder sleeves and tough forged-steel cross-bolted main bearing caps also set the LS7 block apart from its LS2 little brother: the latter features cast-in sleeves and powder-metal main caps. LS7 pistons are cast-aluminum flat-top units that squeeze the air/fuel mixture at an 11.0:1 ratio. On the bottom end is a balanced forged-steel crank, and lubricating all these wildly rotating parts is a competition-type dry-sump oil system, a first for street-going Corvettes.

LS7 heads, too, look like they belong at the track rather than on the street. "We consulted with our Motorsports group on numerous aspects of the cylinder head design," said valvetrain design engineer Jim Hicks. "We adopted some of the latest ideas that have been successful in the Nextel Cup and the American Le Mans series, including valve centerline positions, valve angles, valve sizes, and rocker arm ratio."

"The heads are simply works of mechanical art," added Dave Muscaro. "We left nothing on the table when it came to ensuring the best airflow through the engine."

Less valve angle is crucial to maximizing flow, and the LS7's valves lean away from their ports at only 12 degrees, compared to 15 degrees for their LS2 counterparts. Those tunnel ports are considerably larger than those in the LS2 heads, and they have been precisely massaged for exceptionally high flow. Valve sizes are 2.20 inches for the titanium intake unit, 1.61 for its sodium-filled running mate. Valve lift is a ridiculous 0.591 inch for intake and exhaust. Hydro-formed stainless-steel headers complete things on the exhaust end.

Building the LS7 is a job as unique as the engine itself. Each engine is hand-assembled with care by a single, specially trained technician at GM Powertrain's new 100,000-square-foot Performance Build Center, located in Wixom, Michigan. According to the facility's site manager, Timothy Schag, this intriguing process represents "a premium manufacturing technique for premium products. (It) brings a higher level of quality, because each builder is personally involved in every aspect of the assembly."

Team members at the Build Center were plucked from GM's experimental engine lab in Pontiac, Michigan. Each builder begins the process in Wixom by selecting components at the center's parts supermarket. An LS7 block is mounted on a movable stand, and this stand then travels through about 15 construction stations, each with all the specialized tools required to perform all assembly steps. Builders stay with the same engine throughout these steps and then perform various quality checks at the end. Only about 30 LS7 V-8s are produced in a day doing it this way, but quantity certainly isn't a priority.

"It was important to step away from the high-volume world we all had lived in for so long and soak in the cadence of these specialized environments," continued Schag. "We learned a lot and established a low-volume manufacturing system on par with the world's best niche builders, but we didn't lose sight of the quality practices already in place at GM."

That the Performance Build Center works like a race shop is clearly no coincidence. "In many ways, the LS7 is a racing engine in a street car," concluded Muscaro. "We've taken much of what we've learned over the years from the 7.0-liter C5-R racing program and instilled it here. There really has been nothing else like it offered in a GM production vehicle."

Talk of an even wilder Z06 has been heard as the LS7 makes its mark in 2006. But taking much more power to the streets may well represent a crime—an offense punishable only if someone can catch you at it.

INDEX